General Editor:	David Jollands
Design Director:	Elwyn Blacker
Consultant Authors:	Roy Edwards
	Alan Hibbert
	Jim Hudson
	John Little
	John Mason
	Cleland McVeigh
	Peter Metcalfe
	Beverley Moody
	Patrick Moore
	Keith Porter
	Tim Pridgeon
	Derek Slack
	Ian Soden
	Tony Soper
	Alan Thomas
Research Editor:	Simon Jollands
Design and Production:	BLA Publishing Limited
	Michael Blacker
	Simon Blacker
	Margaret Hickey
	Graeme Little
	Alison Lawrenson
Artists:	Paul Doherty
	Hayward & Martin
	Dennis Knight
	Richard Lewis
	Steve Lings/Linden Artists
	Eric Thomas
	Rosie Vane-Wright

SCIENCE UNIVERSE SERIES

SIGHT, LIGHT AND COLOR

ARCO PUBLISHING, INC.
NEW YORK

Acknowledgements

The publishers wish to thank the following organizations for their invaluable assistance in the preparation of this book.

British Telecom
Canon (UK)
Central Electricity Generating Board
Ford Motor Company
Kodak Museum
NASA
National Film Board of Canada
Philips International
Royal Greenwich Observatory
Royal Smeets Offset
Shell
Sony (UK)
Southern Positives and Negatives (SPAN)
Standard Telephones and Cables
United Nations Organization
US Information Service

Published by Arco Publishing, Inc.
215 Park Avenue South, New York, N.Y. 10003

© BLA Publishing Limited 1984

First published 1984

Library of Congress Cataloging in Publication Data

Main entry under title:

Sight, light, and color

(Science universe series; v. 3)

Includes index.
Summary: Explains the scientific aspects of light, the eye, and color perception discussing their characteristics and interrelationship with each other.

1. Light – Juvenile literature. 2. Vision – Juvenile literature. 3. Color – Juvenile literature. [1. Light. 2. Vision. 3. Color]

I. Arco Publishing   II. Series

QC360.S54   1984   535   83-26645
ISBN 0-668-06177-4

This book was designed and produced by BLA Publishing Limited, Swan Court, East Grinstead, Sussex, England.
A member of the Ling Kee Group
LONDON · HONG KONG · TAIPEI · NEW YORK · SINGAPORE

Phototypeset in Great Britain by Southern Positives and Negatives (SPAN). Color origination by Chris Willcock Reproductions and Premier Graphics. Printed and bound in The Netherlands by Royal Smeets Offset BV, Weert.

Photographic credits

t = top   b = bottom   l = left   r = right   c = centre

Cover photographs: *tl* ZEFA; *tr* Robert Ellis/Rock Library; *bl* Stephen Dalton/NHPA; *bc* Biophoto Associates/NHPA; *br* ZEFA.

Title page: ZEFA

4, 5 Colorsport; 6*l* ZEFA; 6*t*, 7*l* Michael Holford; 7*t*, 8*l*, 8*r* ZEFA; 9*t* Space Frontiers; 9*c* Paul Brierley; 10*l*, 11, 13 ZEFA; 14 Jolpic; 15 ZEFA; 16 Mary Evans Picture Library; 17*t*, 17*b* Patrick Moore Picture Library; 18*bl*, 18*b* Paul Brierley; 18*t*, 19 ZEFA; 22, R. J. Erwin/NHPA; 23*tl* Heather Angel; 23*r*, 23*b* Stephen Dalton/NHPA; 25*l*, 25*b* D. J. Mayer; 26*bc*, 26*bc* Heather Angel; 26*t* Barry Angel/NHPA; 27*l* ZEFA; 27*r* Stephen Dalton/NHPA; 29*t* Michael Holford; 29*r* National Gallery, London; 32*l* ZEFA; 32*t*, 33*l*, 33*r* R. Balharry/NHPA; 34*l* ZEFA; 35*t* Paul Brierley; 35*b* ZEFA; 36*t*, 36*bl*, 36*br* Kodak; 37*t* Michael Holford; 37*c*, 37*b* Kodak; 38*t* Canon; 39*t* US Information Service; 40 Kodak; 41 Philips; 42*l*, 42*r* Kodak; 44, 45 Stephen Dalton/NHPA; 48*l* Mansell Collection; 48*r*, 48/49, 49*t*, 49*b*, 50*l*, 50*r*, 51*t*, 51*b*, 52 ZEFA; 54*t*, 54*l*, 54*r*, 55*t* Paul Brierley; 55*b*, 56 Philips; 57*t*, 57*b* British Telecom; 58 ZEFA; 59 Biophoto Associates/NHPA; 60, 61 Mansell Collection.

Conversion table for units

Length

1 nanometer (nm)	= 0.000001 millimeter	= 0.000000001 meter (one-billionth of a meter)
1 millimeter (mm)	= 0.1 centimeter	= 0.03937 inch
1 centimeter (cm)	= 10 millimeters	= 0.3937 inch
1 meter (m)	= 100 centimeters	= 39.37 inches
1 kilometer (km)	= 1000 meters	= 3280.8 feet = 0.621 mile

Area

1 square kilometer = 0.3861 square mile

Capacity

1 liter = 1.0567 quarts

Volume

1 cubic centimeter (cc) = 0.06102 cubic inch

Weight

1 kilogram (kg)	= 2.2 pounds	
1 metric ton	= 1000 kilograms	= 1.1 US tons

Contents

Introduction	4
Sight and light	6
How light behaves	8
The nature of light	10
Light reflection and mirrors	12
Lenses and the microscope	14
The telescope	16
Newton and the spectrum	18
The human eye	20
Vision in the living world	22
How we see color	24
Color vision in the living world	26
Perspective	28
Perception and optical illusion	30
Display and camouflage	32
The primary colors	34
Light sensitivity	36
How a camera works	38
Developing and printing	40
Motion pictures	42
High-speed and time lapse photography	44
The electromagnetic spectrum	46
Beyond red in the spectrum	48
Beyond violet in the spectrum	50
How a laser works	52
How lasers are used	54
Fibre optics	56
The miracle of sunlight	58
Summary	60
Glossary	62
Index	64

NOTE TO THE READER: while you are reading this book you will notice that certain words appear in **bold type**. This is to indicate a word listed in the Glossary on page 62. This glossary gives brief explanations of words which may be new to you.

Introduction

SINCE it was first formed, the Earth has been bathed in light from the Sun. All life responds to sunlight in one way or another. Because of light, eyes have developed in animals over millions of years, so that they are able to select their food and avoid their enemies. Of all the forms of life on Earth, the human being is probably the one depending most on eyesight. Almost nine-tenths of all the information that reaches our brains comes through our eyes. This makes sight our most important sense, far more than smell, taste, touch or hearing.

Sight, light and color are so much a part of our whole existence that it is all too easy to take them for granted. People who have been blind from birth are cut off from the world of light and color. They cannot tell what something looks like, nor can they know what is meant by color.

In the picture of the Olympic games stadium we can see how light and color play their part. The grass is green because plant leaves take in all the other colors in white light, and they **reflect** green. Close your eyes and imagine what the grass feels like or even smells like. You can do this because in the past you have touched and smelled grass. Your eyes tell you that the green in the picture is grass, and you remember all the other things about grass. This shows that eyes play an important part in learning. You can 'feel' the grass in your imagination without even touching it.

As night draws in, the stadium and the colors in it would become shadowy and dark without floodlights. Artificial lighting is not as perfect as natural sunlight. The grass will appear a slightly different shade of green because the colors that make up man-made light are different from those of sunlight. We can imagine the orange-red street lamps outside the stadium. Under their light the grass verges will look almost black. This is because the grass will **absorb,** or take in the orange-red light and will reflect hardly any light at all.

Colors are important to us as a way of recognizing groups and differences. In the Olympic stadium each nation is represented by a different colored flag. The athletes themselves wear distinctive team colors, so that in a race it is possible to see quickly which nation is in the lead.

Hundreds of millions of spectators all over the world watch the Olympic games on color television. It is the event with the biggest audience of all. This is possible because we have copied the human eye by producing pictures with a camera. The first attempts were in black and white. We had to guess what color the objects

Teams from all over the world march into the arena for the Opening Ceremony of the Munich Olympic games in 1972. Only a chosen few take part, but all the world watches. Without the gifts of sight and light none of this would be possible.

were in the picture. Then came moving pictures, then color photography and finally color television.

These pictures can now be sent to all parts of the world by **satellite,** so that every nation can sit at home and watch their own country competing in the games.

The range of colors you can see in the picture on this page look good but you would notice slight differences if you were able to compare it with the actual scene. This is because our eyes are very good at telling the difference between colors and their shades. After all, nature has had very much longer to perfect the human eye than people have had to invent and perfect the camera.

The quality of our lives depends much upon sight, light and color. In this book, we will be describing what light is and how people and animals see it. Also, you will be able to find out many of the ways in which human beings have used light to improve on nature itself.

The colors of the flags identify the nations and give national pride. Without color vision our lives would be very different, as you can see by looking at the black and white picture.

Sight and light

THE SUN is our nearest star. It is tucked away towards the outer edge of the Milky Way Galaxy. The Sun is vital to us, because the energy it **radiates** supports everything that lives on Earth.

We know today that the Sun is not a flat golden disk or a solid ball of rock, but a whirling cloud of gas. We know that it is not on fire, and we have discovered how its energy is produced. To the earliest people on Earth it was a mystery. They knew they could not live without its light and warmth, but that its heat could be fierce enough to kill them and that its light would blind them if they gazed at it. They understood that the Sun was the single most powerful force in their lives. Many ancient civilizations worshipped the Sun as a god.

The ancient Egyptians worshipped the Sun as one of their gods. An Egyptian priestess is seen here bowing down before the disk of the Sun, which contains the eye of the god Ra.

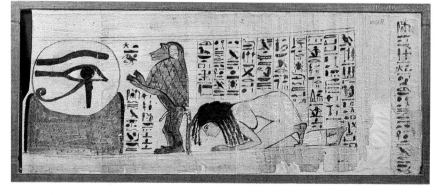

In Egypt it was known as Ra, the greatest of the gods and the creator of life. The Persians worshipped fire, and never allowed the fires in their homes to go out. They thought of the Sun as the greatest of all fires. The Aztecs of Mexico used a symbol of the Sun to stand for 'god' in their writings, and their word for the sky meant 'god-sea'.

When the Sun's power seemed to be failing in autumn and winter, people feared the god was dying. The Romans celebrated the birthday of their Sun-god Mithra at the end of December, when it became clear that the days were getting longer. Their festival was adopted by the Christian church as Christmas.

In the twentieth century we are still 'sun-worshippers'. For most people a 'beautiful day' is one when the sun shines and brightens all the colors of nature. We rush out into the sunshine to feel its warmth on our skin. Everyone feels happier and healthier.

The Sun is the source of nearly all our light. We take it for granted that at sunset we can replace it with artificial light – from candles to fluorescent tubes. But no one has yet managed to invent a light as easy to see by as daylight, even on a cloudy day in winter.

The huge globe of the Sun seen low down in the sky over Lapland. When we see the Sun like this it is hard to believe that the Sun is just an ordinary star.

We need light in order to see. The sense of sight is very important to humans, and is quite highly developed. Our ancestors were **primates**, perhaps something like present-day apes, who lived in trees. Leaping from branch to branch meant that they needed to be very good at judging distances. They also needed good **coordination**, to be able to match the movements of their bodies to the message coming from their eyes. Humans have inherited this skill.

A modern camera can produce a more accurate image than a human eye, but the pictures you see are made by your brain as well as your eyes. The brain adds two extra ingredients to the eyes' image. These are memory and imagination and they are needed to produce a complete picture.

Almost as soon as you were born you began to learn and remember how things look. Your brain does not have to keep figuring out what you are seeing. It recognizes things, and adds what it already knows to each new picture.

Pictures are important to us, and often make a stronger impression than words or sounds can. Most of our dreams are in pictures. We often find that we can remember people's faces although we have forgotten their names.

Humans have always made pictures. The oldest we know of are cave paintings, usually of animals, that are perhaps 30,000 years old. The artists who produced them were very skillful. The paintings are based on what they had observed of the animals' shapes and movements. They are both lifelike and imaginative. Sometimes an animal has been painted around a

The orang utan lives in the trees and feeds on fruit. With long fingers and toes it is almost four-handed. Good vision is important for finding food and judging distances.

bump in the rock of the cave wall. Perhaps the artist looked at this bump and his imagination helped him to see it as a horse or a buffalo.

To imagine something means to picture it in your mind. Humans are so good at this that it is hard to stop your imagination working. You may have noticed this when trying to go to sleep. The first tool was invented when someone looked at a pointed stone and imagined using it to skin an animal or dig a hole. Some animals use sticks and stones as simple tools, but only a human could have had the idea of giving the stone a sharper cutting edge, to make it more useful. The pictures we see in our 'mind's eye' are the beginning of all human inventions, from brick houses to computers.

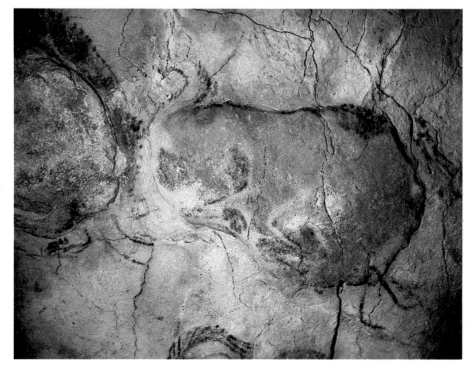

Cave painting of a bison, Altamira, north Spain. The people who lived in caves 30,000 years ago were superb artists. They were able to see in the mind's eye, or imagine, the wild animals which they met when hunting. They probably used materials such as charcoal and clay for their color, which they then mixed with animal fats to produce a paste-like paint.

How light behaves

SIGHT is perhaps the most important of our senses. It is therefore hardly surprising that for many centuries, scientists have studied light itself, which allows us to see things.

On our planet Earth, all animals and plants need light in order to live, and without it they would die. Many early civilizations worshipped the Sun. Since the Sun gives out its own light, it is described as being **luminous.** The Sun has been giving out light for many millions of years. However, like all the other stars in the sky, it will not do so for ever. Very gradually, the Sun's energy is being used up. In several billion years, it will stop producing light. Long before this time, all life on Earth will have ceased to exist.

Light is clearly an important part of our lives. In the seventeenth century, Torricelli noted that light did not need to travel through air to get from one place to another. He owned a barometer, an instrument to measure the pressure of the atmosphere. This barometer contained a column of the element mercury, in a sealed glass tube. At the top of the tube, above the mercury, was a space which contained no air, known as a **vacuum.** Torricelli noted that light passed through the vacuum at the top of his barometer. This showed that light was very different from sound, which is not carried through a vacuum. Torricelli's discovery seems obvious when you realize that the light from the Sun travels almost 150 million km to the Earth, through the vacuum of outer space.

When light strikes any object or surface, it bounces back, just like a ball bouncing off a floor or a wall. This bouncing of light is called **reflection.** A surface such as a black piece of paper reflects very little light. However, the surface of a mirror reflects almost all the light which falls upon it.

Some materials such as glass, cellophane or Plexiglas TM, allow light to pass through them.

This dramatic picture *(below left)* clearly shows that light travels from a source in straight lines. The beams of light are only made visible by dust or moisture in the air.

A laser light beam refracts (is bent) as it passes through a beaker of water. Some of the light is also reflected and does not pass through the glass.

These substances are called **transparent.** However, even with transparent substances, a little light is reflected from the surface, and a little more is **absorbed,** so that not all of the light passes through.

Most people know about the reflection of light. But you can also prove that light can bend sometimes. Fill a large bowl with water and hold a ruler at an angle, so that half is immersed under water, and half of it is above the water. You will notice that the ruler seems to be bent. It appears to bend at the place where it enters the water. Now slowly alter the angle the ruler makes as it enters the water. When the ruler is

Skylab view of the Moon rising over the Earth. The Moon is seen through the upper fringes of the Earth's atmosphere, showing great distortion of the lower part of the Moon. The upper part is not distorted, since light is not refracted or bent in the vacuum of outer space.

The left-hand glass contains water to the top and the image of the spoon is refracted. The right-hand glass has no water and there is no refraction.

Although sound waves can go around corners, light rays cannot. We know this to be true when we see a shadow cast by a source of light such as the Sun.

upright, it does not appear to bend at all. However, as you tilt the ruler over, it seems to bend more and more. The ruler is, of course, really perfectly straight. The apparent bending of the ruler where it enters the water is called **refraction.** The ruler appears bent because the direction in which light is travelling can be changed when it passes from air into water. In fact, refraction occurs whenever light passes from one transparent substance into another. Examples are, from air into water and from air into glass.

Whenever light is travelling through a transparent substance, it appears to travel in straight lines. The distance the light has to travel makes no difference to this fact. The light passing from an electric bulb to the page of a book several centimeters away, will follow a straight line. So also does the light from the Sun, as it travels across space to the Earth.

A beam of light cannot travel around corners. Instead it casts shadows. Everyone has at some time seen their own shadow. It might have been on a bright sunny day, or at nighttime when standing in the light of a street lamp. Substances which do not allow light to pass through them are called **opaque.** A shadow is cast when an opaque object is placed in a beam of light.

The nature of light

WHAT IS LIGHT? After many centuries of study, and thousands of experiments, scientists still find it very difficult to give a simple explanation. In attempting to understand what light is, we have a problem, because light is invisible; we cannot see it. You might find it difficult to understand how light itself can be invisible. However, a simple experiment will prove to you that this is so.

Find a cardboard box, about the size of a shoebox. Make two cardboard tubes about 10 cm long and 3 cm in diameter. Then cut a circular hole in the exact center of each end of the box, also 3 cm in diameter. Paint the insides of box and tubes with black watercolor paint. Push the tubes into the holes at each end of the box. Fix them in with tape, and make sure there are no holes elsewhere. Glue down the lid of the box firmly. Finally, cut a window in the side of the box, and cover the window with a piece of transparent plastic.

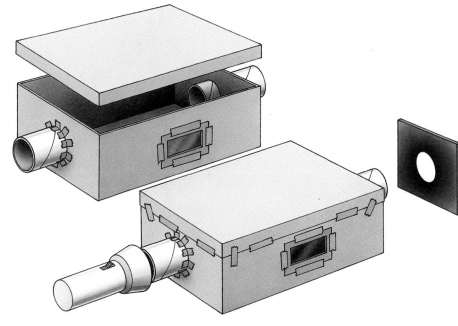

Take the box into a darkened room and put it on a table. Shine a flashlight into one of the tubes and hold a piece of white cardboard a short distance away from the opposite tube. You will see that the flashlight light reaches the piece of white card. However, if you look through the window of the box you will see – nothing! The beam of light from the flashlight is invisible. Outer space is like the inside of the box, total darkness.

Light must be reflected from something before it can be seen. When light from the Sun reaches the Earth, it enters our atmosphere. Here it is reflected by millions of tiny **particles** of dust or water droplets. As these reflect the light, they give color to the sky and to the clouds above us. Next time you go to the movies, look up at the beam of light passing from the projector to the screen. Inside this beam, you will see the glint of millions of tiny dust particles floating around in the air. Each of these dust particles is reflecting the light. This allows you to see the beam.

For several thousands of years scientists have thought about the nature of light. The ancient

The Pantheon, in Rome, was built about 120 AD. Its only source of light is a circular opening at the top of the dome. You can see the beam of sunlight reflected by the dust particles.

Greeks carried out the first experiments. Euclid, in the third century BC, knew about the reflection of light. Ptolemy, a century later, investigated the refraction of light as it passed from one transparent substance to another.

In the late seventeenth century, Isaac Newton attempted to explain the properties of light. He suggested that a light beam consisted of a stream of tiny particles. He called these **corpuscles.** His theory explained the fact that light travelled in straight lines. He also thought that the reflection of light by a mirror took place as the corpuscles bounced off the surface of the mirror. Newton thought that the corpuscles were attracted to certain transparent substances and moved faster in them. This was his explanation of refraction. When light passes from air into water it is bent. Newton thought that the amount of bending depended upon how much faster the corpuscles travelled in water or glass compared to air.

Newton thought there were different kinds of corpuscle for each of the many colors of light. The corpuscles of one color were all the same. However, they were different from those of another color.

In about 1690, a Dutch physicist, Christiaan

Wavelength is the distance between the top, or crest, of one wave to the crest of the wave next to it. Frequency is the number of crests passing a point in one second of time.

When a pebble, or a raindrop, falls on water a ripple of waves moves out from the center. The waves of light would be so small that they would rise and fall, or ripple several hundred thousand billion times every second.

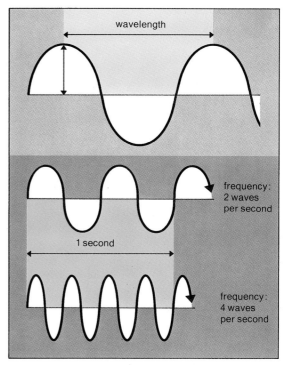

Huygens, put forward a new idea. Unlike Newton, he thought that light travelled as **waves.** If you drop a pebble into water, you will see that waves or ripples move out from the place where the pebble hits the water. Huygens believed that light travelled in a similar way but that the waves were very small. This distance between the tops of any two neighboring waves is only a few ten-thousandths of a millimeter. This minute measurement is called the **wavelength** of the light. The waves of light rise and fall several hundred thousand billion times every second. This is called the **frequency** of the light waves.

Although Huygens' theory explained reflection, refraction and several other properties of light, it took more than a century for his ideas to win support. The important difference between the two theories of Newton and Huygens was that Huygens' theory needed light to travel more slowly in glass or water, than in air. Newton predicted the opposite. Finally, in 1850, Foucault showed that light travelled slower in water than in air. Huygens was right, and Newton was wrong.

Earlier this century, Albert Einstein proposed that light travelled through space at a definite speed. The speed of light is about 300,000 km per second. Einstein also believed that light waves actually consisted of individual 'packets' of light **energy.** He called these **photons.** In some ways, light behaves as a wave. In others it behaves as though it consists of particles. No longer are the two explanations by Newton and Huygens thought of as rival theories.

Light reflection and mirrors

WE HAVE SEEN that light is reflected from all surfaces upon which it falls, just as a ball bounces off a floor or wall. This is very important, because when light is reflected from objects into our eyes, we are able to see them. If you bounce a ball on a smooth floor it returns directly to your hand in a straight upward bounce. However, if you do the same thing on a rough, uneven surface such as a gravel path, it is likely to bounce off at any angle. Each time you bounce the ball it may go in a different direction. Light, too, is reflected in a different way from smooth and rough surfaces. However, the reflection of light is also affected by the color and the type of surface which it strikes.

Even with transparent substances, which allow light to pass through them, a little light will be reflected from the surface. Also, a little light will be absorbed as it passes through the transparent material. An opaque substance allows no light to pass through it. If light falls upon an opaque surface, some of it is absorbed and the rest is reflected. The amount of light absorbed depends on the color of the object. White or very light objects reflect a lot of light and absorb very little. Dark colors absorb most of the light and reflect very little.

Apart from its color, the kind of surface is important; in other words, is it rough or smooth? Look at a sheet of plain white cardboard on a bright sunny day. It will shine too brightly for your eyes. The light is easily reflected by the white surface. Also the cardboard is smooth and the light is reflected directly upwards, just like bouncing a ball on a smooth surface. Now, take a dark-colored sponge and look at it on the same sunny day. The sponge will not reflect light in the same way as the white cardboard. The dull surface absorbs some of the light. Also the rough texture of the sponge will scatter the light in all directions. Very little will be reflected directly upwards. This is similar to bouncing a ball on a gravel path.

One of the easiest ways to reflect light is by

A submarine periscope uses the principle of light reflection. In this diagram two 45 degree glass prisms each bend the light through 90 degrees. You can make a simple periscope by using two flat mirrors and a hollow tube. Like the prisms, the mirrors should be set at angles of 45 degrees.

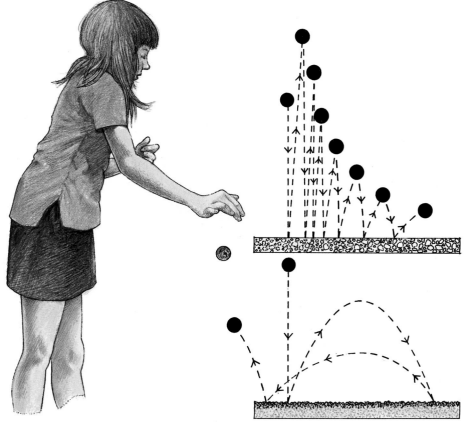

Light behaves in a similar way to the bouncing ball in these two diagrams. The way it is reflected varies according to the nature of the surface that it strikes, just like the ball. The upper diagram shows the effect from an even surface such as smooth concrete. The lower shows the effect of an uneven surface such as gravel.

using a mirror. This is a piece of glass with a very thin layer of shiny metal, usually fixed to the rear surface. We know that light travels in a straight line, and because of this we cannot see round corners. Unless, of course, you happen to have a mirror. A flat mirror allows you to see around corners by bouncing the light off at an angle to that in which it was originally travelling. By using two flat mirrors, you can make yourself a **periscope.** With this, you can see over walls or look over people's heads if you are in the middle of a crowd.

If you stand in front of a large flat mirror you will see an **image** of yourself. Look carefully at yourself in the mirror and you will notice something interesting. Close your right eye. You will see that it appears in the mirror as though you have closed your left eye. Similarly, if you raise your right arm it will look as though you have moved your left arm. It appears as though your whole body has been reversed so that left has become right and right has become left. In other words, the image you see of yourself in a mirror is not the same as your friends see you. This experiment can be repeated if you write your name on a piece of cardboard and hold this up to the mirror. Again, you will see that the letters appear to be reversed.

When you stand in front of a mirror, your image does not appear to come from the surface of the mirror. Walk up to a mirror so that your nose is touching the glass. Then walk slowly backwards, and your image will appear to be moving further and further behind the mirror. If you walk forward again, your image moves towards you, closer to the surface of the mirror. In fact, your image is the same distance behind the mirror as you are in front of it.

If you place an alarm clock in front of a small flat mirror, its image will again appear to be reversed. Now get a second mirror as near as possible in size and shape to the first. Stand the

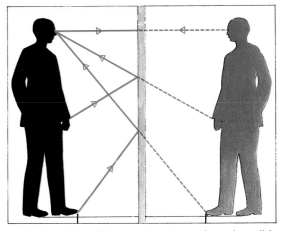

The paths of three light rays have been shown by solid lines as they reflect off the mirror to the eye. The dotted lines show a continuation of the reflected rays as seen by the eye. As a result the image appears to be behind the mirror.

two mirrors up at right angles to each other with their back edges touching. The corners of this book are a right angle. You can use it to help angle the mirrors correctly. If you now place the clock in front of the two mirrors, it will no longer appear reversed. The light from the right side of the clock is reflected by the right mirror into the left mirror and back to your eyes. Also, light from the left of the clock is reflected by the left mirror into the right mirror and from there to your eyes. This double reflection reverses the

image and then reverses it again, so that the image of the clock appears normal.

Not all mirrors are flat; some are curved. Find a large polished dinner spoon and hold it as you would if you were eating. The bowl of the spoon makes a **concave** mirror. Your image will appear upside down in the bowl of the spoon. Now turn the spoon over and look at your reflection in the underside of the bowl. This makes a **convex** mirror. Your image will no longer be upside down. You might also notice that the convex mirror reflects much more of the room around you; this is called wide-angle vision. Some amusement parks have mirrors which have very complicated curved surfaces. These produce very strange and rather funny images of people standing in front of them.

The left hand picture shows the effect of a single reflection. A double reflection (right) causes an object to be seen the correct way round. Note the careful positioning of the two mirrors in relation to the clock.

Light is being distorted in different directions by this mirror. It has a wavy surface deliberately designed to distort the image, giving the curious effect.

Lenses and the microscope

MOST PEOPLE at one time or another will have looked through a **lens.** Whenever you use a magnifying glass, a pair of binoculars, eyeglasses or a microscope, you are looking through one or more lenses. A lens is made of transparent material and this is normally glass. A lens always has one or both of its surfaces curved. Depending on how the lens surfaces are curved, it is called either convex or concave. A convex lens is thicker in the middle than it is at the edges. A concave lens is thinner in the middle than at the edges.

To understand how lenses work, we need to see how an extremely thin beam of light, known as a **ray** of light, behaves as it passes through a lens. When a light ray passes from the air into a lens it is refracted. In other words, the direction in which the light ray was travelling is changed as it enters the glass from the air. The light ray then passes through the lens. As it leaves the glass lens on the other side, and enters the air, it is refracted once again. These two refractions of the light ray and the **curvature** of the two lens surfaces, cause the ray to be 'bent' one way or the other.

With a convex lens, a ray of light passing through the exact center of the lens will be unaffected. However, rays entering the lens further from the center will be bent inwards. As a result, a broad beam of light falling upon a convex lens will be made to **converge**, so that all the light is concentrated at one point. Most people know what happens if the Sun's rays are directed through a convex lens onto a piece of paper. The convex lens bends the light so that it collects at one point, called the **focus** of the lens. You will know how bright the spot is where the

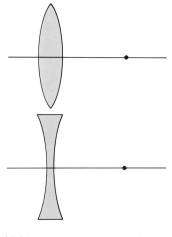

Light rays passing through the exact center of a convex lens *(top)* or a concave lens *(bottom)* travel in a straight line.

rays of sunlight are concentrated into a tiny space. Rays of heat and light are very much alike. They behave the same way when passed through a convex lens. This is the reason why the paper burns when the Sun's rays are focused at one point. For any convex lens, the distance between the focus and the center of the lens is called the **focal length.** You will find that thick convex lenses usually have a shorter focal length than thin convex lenses.

It should now be clear why you must never look through a lens, directly at the Sun. When using a convex lens as a 'burning glass' the heat is concentrated at the focus. If you were foolish enough to look through a lens at the Sun, the heat would be concentrated on the back of your eye. Blindness would almost certainly result.

A magnifying glass has a single convex lens, which bends light rays inwards. Here the Sun's rays can be seen passing through a glass to a focus of bright light, strong enough in this case to burn a hole in the paper.

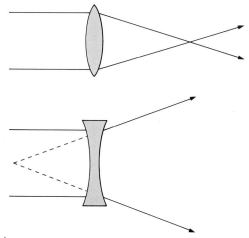

The convex lens *(top)* bends light rays inwards, which meet at a focus. The more curved the lens, the more the rays are bent. The concave lens *(bottom)* makes light rays spread outwards, or diverge.

Stand inside a window on a sunny day. Allow the light rays from the window to pass through a convex lens and on to a piece of white cardboard. By moving the lens towards or away from the cardboard you will be able to produce a clear, bright image of the window on the cardboard. This image will be upside down. We call such an image a **real image.** When you stand in front of a mirror, you see an image of yourself. However, this image could not be obtained on a piece of white cardboard held behind the mirror. We call this a **virtual image.**

A convex lens may be used as a magnifying

glass, or simple microscope. This is because it will make objects appear larger when held at a certain distance away from them. We wish the image to be the same way up as it appears with the unaided eye. So when using a magnifying glass you must put the object to be viewed between the lens and the focus. Rays of light reflected from the object, pass through the lens to the eye. When these rays enter the eye it sees a virtual image behind the magnifying glass. This image is magnified, that is, made larger than the original object. The magnification of any microscope is how much larger the image appears to the eye, compared with the original object. A magnifying glass, with a magnification of two and a half times (written 2.5 ×) would produce a virtual image which appeared two and a half times larger than the object.

This diagram shows how an object appears bigger when seen through a magnifying glass. The eye sees the rays that have been bent by the lens; the image that these rays produce is in fact further away than the object itself.

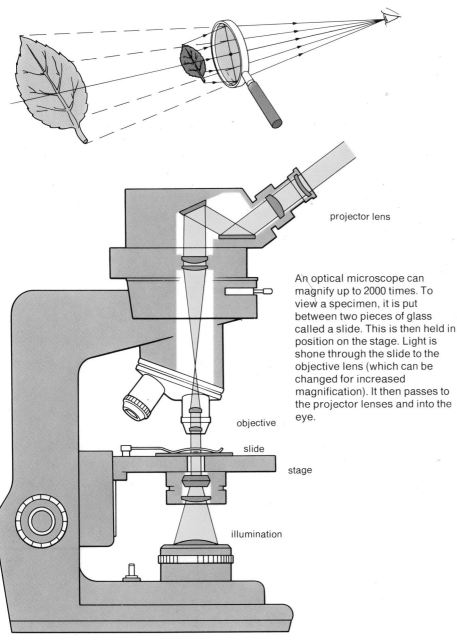

projector lens

An optical microscope can magnify up to 2000 times. To view a specimen, it is put between two pieces of glass called a slide. This is then held in position on the stage. Light is shone through the slide to the objective lens (which can be changed for increased magnification). It then passes to the projector lenses and into the eye.

objective

slide

stage

illumination

An early compound microscope, circa 1680. Since its invention in 1590 the microscope has proved a valuable tool to scientists, especially biologists. The first microscopes had only two lenses but modern ones use more to give higher magnification and a sharper image.

To obtain very high magnifications, a simple magnifying glass cannot be used. The highly magnified image must be produced in two stages. This is done in a **compound** microscope. It consists of two lenses; one called the **objective**, the other called the **eyepiece**. This type of microscope will provide a magnification of greater than 30 ×, of nearby objects. The objective lens, which is closest to the object, forms a real image of the object. It will be upside down. The eyepiece then magnifies this image still further. The eye sees a virtual image which is still upside down.

So far, we have talked about convex lenses. With a concave lens, a ray of light passing through the exact center of the lens is again unaffected. However, rays entering the lens further from the center will be bent outwards. As a result, a broad beam of light falling upon a concave lens will be made to diverge. The light will not be concentrated at one point, but will be spread out over an area larger than the original beam. A concave lens cannot be used as a magnifying glass. This is because it makes objects appear smaller and not larger. This type of lens does not have so many uses as the convex. However, they are used in the eyeglasses of short or near-sighted people.

The telescope

IT IS NOT CLEAR who invented the telescope. In fact, it may have been invented and re-invented many times. By the beginning of the seventeenth century, eyeglass lenses had been in use in Europe for roughly three hundred years. During that time it is more than likely that on several occasions two eyeglass lenses might have been arranged, purely by chance, to form a telescope.

The earliest records show that by October 1608, a Dutch eyeglass maker named Hans Lippershey had built a telescope. He called it a 'device for seeing at a distance', which is what the word *teleskopos* means in Greek. From this we get our modern word telescope. The Italian astronomer Galileo Galilei heard about the invention. By 1609 he had made a telescope of his own, using two lenses and an organ pipe as a tube. Later, he built a number of better telescopes. At the beginning of 1610, Galileo turned his first telescope skywards. He discovered the moons of Jupiter, saw Saturn's rings, and observed **sunspots**.

There are two types of telescope; refracting telescopes and reflecting telescopes. A refracting telescope uses only lenses. A reflecting telescope uses both mirrors and lenses. The Galilean telescope consists of one convex and one concave lens. The more common astronomical refracting telescope consists of two convex lenses. In each case, the lens nearest the

Three types of refractor. (1) Galilean, (2) simple astronomical refractor, (3) terrestrial refractor. Terrestrial telescopes are used for looking at objects on Earth.

The Newtonian reflector (4). Light passes down a tube to a concave mirror which reflects the light back to a smaller, flat mirror set at an angle of 45°. The image on that mirror is magnified by the eyepiece.

object is called the **objective**. The lens nearest the eye of the observer is called the **eyepiece**. The refracting telescope can be compared to a compound microscope. The main difference between the two is the distance of the object to be viewed. A compound microscope is used to produce a magnified image of a nearby object. This is always close to the objective lens. The telescope is used to obtain a magnified image of a distant object.

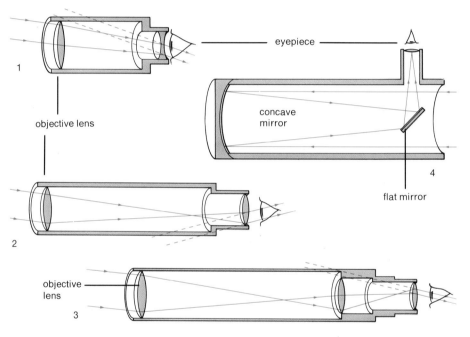

The Galilean telescope produced a virtual image which was the same way up as the distant object. The lenses in the Galilean telescope are much closer together than those in the astronomical telescope consisting of two convex lenses. For this reason, the Galilean instrument is much shorter and is used in opera glasses. The eyepiece of the Galilean telescope is the concave lens. For best results, the eye should be as close as possible to the eyepiece. This means that the field of view is very limited, compared to that of the other astronomical refractor. This is the main disadvantage of the Galilean telescope.

In this old print, Galileo is seen showing Jupiter's satellites to senators of Venice. He also used his telescope to look closely at the Moon, observing the mountains and craters.

The simple astronomical **refractor** with two convex lenses produces a virtual image which is upside down. This is not a problem when using the telescope for astronomy, because it makes little difference if a star, for example, appears upside down. However, if you want to look at distant objects on the earth or sea, this is inconvenient. So a third convex lens is added between the objective and the eyepiece. The instrument is now called a terrestrial refracting telescope. The virtual image produced is the same way up as the distant object. This is called an **erect image**. The third lens is therefore known as the erecting lens of the telescope. This third lens absorbs some light (as do all lenses) and this is a disadvantage. Another disadvantage is that it increases the length of the telescope tube.

For astronomical purposes, mirrors are often used instead of some of the lenses, to produce a reflecting telescope. This type of telescope was invented by a Scotsman, James Gregory, in 1661. Isaac Newton constructed the first successful reflecting telescope in 1668. He used two mirrors and an eyepiece. The objective in the Newtonian reflector is a concave mirror. This collects the light and brings it to a focus. A small flat mirror is used to direct the beam from the concave mirror out to the side of the tube. It is here that an eyepiece may be fixed. William Herschel used a reflecting telescope in the eighteenth century. The mirrors in a reflecting

The multiple mirror telescope at Mount Hopkins, Arizona, was completed in 1978.

telescope use a thin layer of silver or aluminum as their reflecting surface. This is deposited on the front surface of the mirror glass.

Reflecting telescopes have become very important. As astronomers try to look at fainter and still more distant objects, it is important to collect as much light as possible. This means that the objective lens, or concave mirror of a reflecting telescope, should be as large as possible. Unfortunately, large lenses are extremely difficult to make. The glass must be highly transparent and free from bubbles. Some light will be lost as it is absorbed by the glass. A lens can only be supported around its edge, and it may sag under its own weight. However, a front-surfaced mirror may be made of poorer quality glass. It may be supported not only by its edge, but also all over its back as well. No light is absorbed by a mirror, and all colours of light are reflected equally. This is unlike a lens which refracts different colours to a different extent.

The world's largest refracting telescope is the 1.02-m Yerkes telescope at Williams Bay, Wisconsin. The two largest reflecting telescopes are the 5.1-m Hale reflector on Mount Palomar, in the U.S., and the 6-m reflector of the Crimean Observatory, in the Soviet Union. Telescopes are also being put into space. Here they can view the stars without interference from the Earth's atmosphere. The atmosphere absorbs a lot of light and causes the image to be unsteady. The space telescope that will be launched by the Space Shuttle has a main mirror 2.4 m in diameter. It is capable of outperforming all of the Earth-based telescopes, although it is smaller.

The multiple mirror telescope. In this new kind of telescope, a group of six 1.8-m reflectors are mounted around one 0.76-m reflector. This acts as a guide telescope. The light from the six reflectors is fed to a central focus. A laser beam is used to keep the six reflectors in line.

Newton and the spectrum

HAVE YOU EVER THOUGHT how dull everything would look if there were no colors? Think of the brightly colored flowers, birds and butterflies. Also, airplanes, ships, trains and cars all have their different colors. Colored lights are an important part of our lives. Everyone knows the red, yellow and green colors of the traffic lights. These control the movement of millions of cars every day.

If you stand in a darkened room, you cannot see any colors. They are not visible in darkness, but can only be produced by light. It was Isaac Newton who first investigated how colored light could be made from white light. In 1665, Newton was doing some experiments with lenses he had made himself. He noticed that the images formed by his lenses were not clear. They seemed blurred and surrounded by a narrow fringe of colored light. However, images produced by curved mirrors were very clear, with no blurring. Newton made more lenses, taking great care when polishing them. He always met the same problem and finally concluded that the fault was not with the lenses. Instead, he thought it was something to do with the refraction of light itself.

Newton carried out more tests. He allowed a narrow beam of sunlight, about 8 mm across, to enter a darkened room, through a small hole in the window-blind. He obtained an image of the Sun on a white screen about 5 m away. When he placed a triangular glass **prism** in the light beam, the rays were bent upwards. Newton observed that the image on the screen was stretched out into a broad band or oblong. This

A secondary rainbow is only visible when the diameter of the raindrops is large enough. It is always fainter than the primary bow and the colors of the spectrum are reversed in order.

appeared to be colored at the ends. Other experiments using a narrow slit, showed Newton that the image was actually made up of a number of overlapping colored patches in place of the white patch.

Newton noted seven different colors in his band of colored light, which we now call a **spectrum.** The colors were red, orange, yellow, green, blue, indigo and violet. By separating each of the seven main colors from the rest, Newton showed that the colors themselves could not be changed by refraction through a further prism. Newton then allowed the whole spectrum to fall on another prism. This was placed the opposite way up to the first prism. A

Isaac Newton's experiment in 1665 was something like this reconstruction *(far left)*. Using a prism, he succeeded in breaking up white light into the colors of the spectrum. In another of his experiments *(left)*, he used two prisms and showed that the colors could be bent back again to produce white light.

white image was obtained. If just one color was removed from the spectrum before passing it into this second prism, it did not produce white light. Newton realized that sunlight, or white light, was a mixture of seven different colors.

Why is white light separated into its main colors by a prism? Each color of light is travelling as a wave, which has a different wavelength. The wavelength of red light is seven ten-thousandths of a millimeter. The wavelength of violet light is four ten-thousandths of a millimeter. When passing into the glass prism, the movement of the waves is hindered. They travel more slowly in glass than in air. As a result each color is bent or refracted. The color with the longest wavelength (red) is bent the least. That with the shortest wavelength (violet) is bent the most. This is because violet light waves travel more slowly through glass than red light waves. The more slowly the colored wave travels through the prism, then the more it is bent or refracted.

You do not have to use a prism to see a spectrum. Most people have at some time or other seen a spectrum formed by a rainbow. Here the spectrum is made by the refraction and reflection of sunlight inside raindrops in the sky. This happens when the Sun breaks through the clouds and starts to shine brightly, while rain is still falling. A sphere of water such as a raindrop can 'break up' white light into its various colors just like a prism. You need to have the Sun behind you, and be looking towards the raindrops to see a rainbow clearly.

The inside of each raindrop acts like a mirror. It reflects sunlight back into your eyes. However, different colors of light are refracted differently as they pass through the water of the raindrop. This means that different colors will be reflected off the back surface of the raindrop at different angles. When only one reflection

Rainbow seen at Niagara Falls.

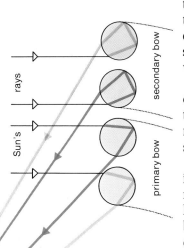

A rainbow is visible when rays of the Sun are refracted and reflected by raindrops, which act like tiny prisms. The light rays are refracted as they enter near the top of a raindrop. They then reflect off the back of the drop and are refracted again when emerging. A secondary bow is formed when light enters near the bottom of the raindrop. Two reflections take place inside the drop. Since the rays cross over twice inside the drop the colors are reversed when they emerge.

takes place inside the raindrop, a **primary rainbow** is formed. This has the strongest colors. You will notice that the outer edge of the bow is red, and the inner edge violet. Sometimes, two or more reflections occur inside raindrops, forming two or more rainbows. A **secondary rainbow**, caused by two reflections, will appear above the primary bow in the sky.

However, its colors will be in the opposite order, with the inner edge appearing red, and the outer one violet. The colors in this bow are not so brilliant as in the primary bow, because some light is lost at every reflection.

Since every raindrop can split the sunlight into a spectrum, you may wonder why we do not see thousands of tiny rainbows. Scientists have found that we are only able to see the bands of color which we call a rainbow at certain positions or angles in the sky. These angles are related to the exact path of the different colors of light through each raindrop and back to your eyes. No two people can see exactly the same rainbow. The water droplets forming a rainbow for one person, will not be the same droplets as those causing the bow seen by another person standing nearby. A rainbow may also be seen when sunlight shines directly into the spray of water droplets from a large waterfall or a fountain. Sometimes, pieces of broken glass, crystals, and gemstones such as diamonds give off sparkles of color. This is because they are acting like small prisms.

The human eye

EYES are one of the most important parts of our body. Through our eyes we can tell the color, size and shape of an object. When we look at a picture or a book we can only see a small part at a time. Try this for yourself by looking at a word on this page. If you keep looking at the same word, notice that the rest of the page is blurred. Normally our eyes do not stay fixed on one point but quickly move over the page or picture. This is almost an optical **illusion** because we are led to think that all the page is equally clear or in **focus.**

In some ways the eye acts like a camera. The clear picture from a camera is produced by moving the lens nearer or further away from the film. The eye has a special type of lens called the **crystalline** lens. Instead of moving this lens back and forward, the eye focuses the picture by changing the shape of the crystalline lens. This is possible because the lens is made from a clear rubbery material and can be moved by tiny muscles.

Just like a camera, the eye can control the amount of light passing through the lens. If you look into a mirror at one of your own eyes you will see the light control, or **iris.** This is the

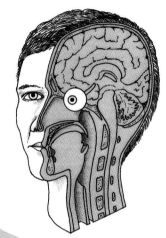

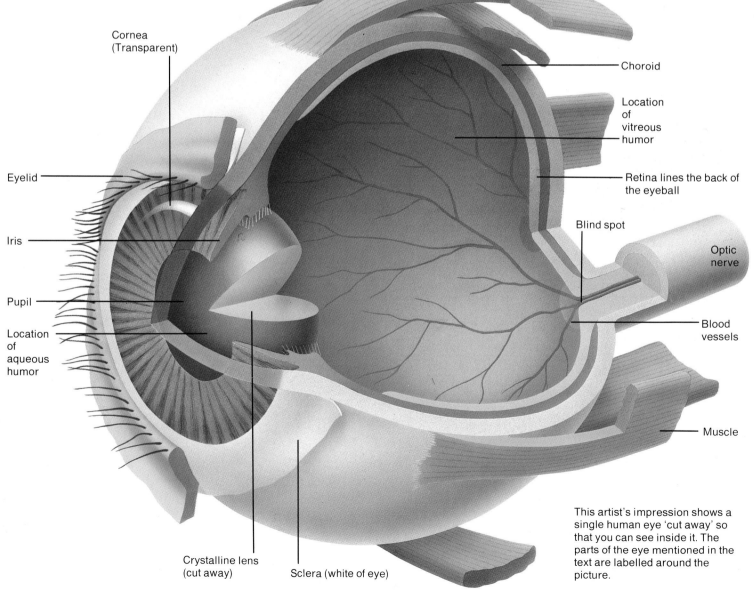

Cornea (Transparent)

Eyelid

Iris

Pupil

Location of aqueous humor

Crystalline lens (cut away)

Sclera (white of eye)

Choroid

Location of vitreous humor

Retina lines the back of the eyeball

Blind spot

Optic nerve

Blood vessels

Muscle

This artist's impression shows a single human eye 'cut away' so that you can see inside it. The parts of the eye mentioned in the text are labelled around the picture.

colored ring which has a dark hole or **pupil** in its center. The iris is a ring of muscle which can change the size of the pupil. It is the part of the eye which is colored blue, green or brown. The pupil is dark because we are looking right through the lens into the eyeball. On a bright day the pupil closes down and is tiny. This reduces the light entering the eye. In the evening the pupil opens right up to let in as much light as possible.

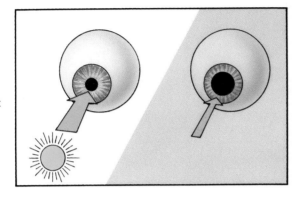

The pupil is the hole through the iris, here shown as blue. In bright light the iris expands across the pupil to reduce the light. Not so much light is needed. When it is dark the iris contracts and opens up the pupil; the eye needs all the light it can get.

The white of the eye, or **sclera**, is a tough skin that covers all the eyeball except for the part over the iris. Here the sclera is clear, forming a protective window called the **cornea.** This keeps dust and dirt out of the lens. The cornea also acts as a very simple lens and bends the light rays towards the crystalline lens. There are no bones in the eye to keep its shape. Instead, the inside of the eyeball is filled with a clear jelly-like liquid called **vitreous humor.** The gap between the cornea and the lens is filled with a watery fluid known as **aqueous humor.**

Now we know how light enters the eye and is focused into a clear picture or image by the lens. How is this image seen by the brain? The inside of the eyeball is lined with special nerve cells which produce signals or **impulses** when light is shone on them. This inner lining is called the retina. Between the retina and the outside of the eyeball is a dark colored layer called the **choroid.** This dark layer stops light reflecting back into the eye just as the black paint on the inside of a camera body stops reflection.

There are two main types of cell in the retina, called **rods** and **cones** because of their shape. These are special nerve cells which send impulses to the brain. When light is shone into the eye it reaches the rods and cones through a thin layer of transparent nerve fibres. These fibres collect at the back of the eye to form the **optic nerve.** At the point where this large nerve leaves the eye there are no rods or cones and so this point is known as the **blind spot.** Only cones are sensitive to colors, the rods can only 'see' in shades of grey.

Close your left eye and look at the left dot with your right eye. Now slowly bring the page closer. When it is about 30 cm away the right dot disappears. This happens when the image on your retina falls on the blind spot.

Each eye is protected from injury by being set in a hard bony hollow in the skull. Our eyelids also give protection from dust, rain and other such things. Every time we blink the upper eyelids wash a drop of liquid over the eye. This liquid comes from the **tear gland** under each eyelid and contains an antiseptic which stops infection.

If the eyeball is altered in shape through strain or old age, the image produced by the lens is fuzzy. If we have difficulty seeing near objects we are said to be farsighted. If distant objects are blurred then we are nearsighted. These faults can be corrected by wearing eyeglasses with special lenses. Contact lenses are similar but are made to fit over the surface of the eye itself.

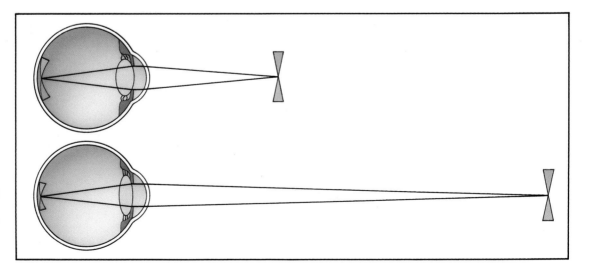

When you are looking at a distant object, the lens of your eye thins out and the object appears small. When looking at a close object, the lens thickens and the object appears large.

Vision in the living world

WE CAN SEE quite clearly with one eye, so why do we need two? Our eyes cannot be used to look in different directions at once. They work as a pair. Whatever you look at, your brain makes just one picture from the information it is given by both your eyes.

Special cells in the brain combine the two images to give us **binocular vision.** This means that we can tell the distance of an object and what shape it is. If you had only one eye, the world would look flat, as it is in a photograph. You would be seeing it in two dimensions. With two eyes, we are able to see in three dimensions.

Binocular vision helps us judge distances. The brain does this by measuring how much our eyes **converge** on an object. Our eyes turn inwards more when we look at something close than when it is far off.

Judging distances works best when the eyes both look forward from the front of the head. To work well the eyes must also be quite far apart. The owl has eyes on the front of its head but has to bob its head from side to side to judge distance. Apart from ourselves, the best binocular vision is found in monkeys living in trees. They need to judge distances as they leap from branch to branch. Like humans, they use their hands to hold and examine objects and need good forward vision to see these. Hunting animals also have eyes at the front of their heads. For instance, a cat chasing a mouse must know exactly when to pounce.

With eyes at the front, the area an animal can see without moving its head is quite narrow. We call this its field of vision. If you hold your hands in front of your face you can see them clearly. Move them round to your sides (still looking straight ahead) and they soon become a blur. Birds need to have a wide field of vision so that they can see the approach of a cat or fox. The woodcock has eyes sticking out from the sides of its head. As a result, it has a field of vision that covers a full circle.

Some animals have far sharper sight than humans. Many birds need to see well from great distances. In particular, hawks look for mice on the ground while hovering high in the sky. Their eyes are about eight times sharper than our eyes. This is because they have cones only in one area of the retina. The cones produce much sharper pictures than the other type of retina cell, the rod. Elephants have very few visual cells. They see near objects as blurred and can hardly see distant things at all.

Galapagos Hawk hovering *(opposite).* Hawks look for their prey while hovering at some height. Their vision is about eight times sharper than ours.

The Screech Owl. Owls are nocturnal and hunt for their prey after dark. The very large pupils of their eyes open wide to let in as much light as possible.

In the diagram below, the primate *(left)* has good binocular vision and a good forward field of vision. The woodcock *(right)* has eyes in the side of its head. This gives poor forward binocular and some binocular vision behind the head. It has a very good all-round field of vision.

Creatures such as owls, cats and bats that are active at night, are called **nocturnal** animals. Their eyes contain mainly rods, which are the cells that can work in dim light, but produce only a black and white image. To help night vision their very large pupils open wide to let in as much light as possible. During the day the pupils shrink to pin holes which protect their eyes from bright light.

Humans and other **vertebrates** have eyes with a single lens and millions of visual cells. Insects have **compound** eyes that are the opposite of this. They have thousands of lenses, each directing light to only a few cells. Each segment of this sort of eye is called an **ommatidium** (plural ommatidia), and is divided from the others by black pigment which can stop light passing from one segment to the next. This pigment moves up and down the omma-

The compound eyes of the Aeshna dragonfly almost surround its head. For catching insects in the air it needs very accurate vision.

A cross section of a single ommatidium *(below)* from an insect's compound eye. Some insects have as many as 25,000 ommatidia.

Chameleons have eyes which do not move together like ours. The eyes swivel independently, allowing them to look in two directions at once. They also have a much wider field of view and, without moving the head, can see above, below and behind.

tidium to control the amount of light entering each segment or **facet.** The pigment is doing the same job as the pupil of our eye.

A bee's eye contains about 15,000 ommatidia and its field of vision is divided into tiny areas. The bee notices movement when either light or shade passes over one area to another. It can also work out its direction to and from the hive by making sure it always sees the sun through the same part of its eye. Some insect eyes can do two jobs at the same time. There are some water beetles with eyes split into two parts, a lower part to see under the water, and an upper half to see up into the sky.

How we see color

ONLY HUMANS and a few other animals like monkeys can see color. It is strange to think that most other animals do not see the world as we do. The secret of how we can see in color is found in the light sensitive lining of each eyeball, called the retina. Light is focused by the lens of the eye on to tiny light sensitive cells, or **receptors**, which make up the retina. There are two types of receptor in the retina. These are called rods and cones because of their shape. In a single eye there may be as many as one hundred and twenty million rods and seven million cones. You can imagine how small each must be to fit into the retina.

The rods are not important in color vision as they only produce black and white pictures. Each rod contains a colored chemical called a **pigment**. This pigment is sensitive to light and sets up a small electric current when light is shone on it. It works in a similar way to **solar cells** which produce electricity when the sun shines on them. The pigment in rods is sensitive to all colors and works well in dim light. For example, the rods are used for seeing at night. Cones need much brighter light to work well and are used for daytime vision. The next time you are outside when it is getting dark, notice how everything looks colorless. This is because

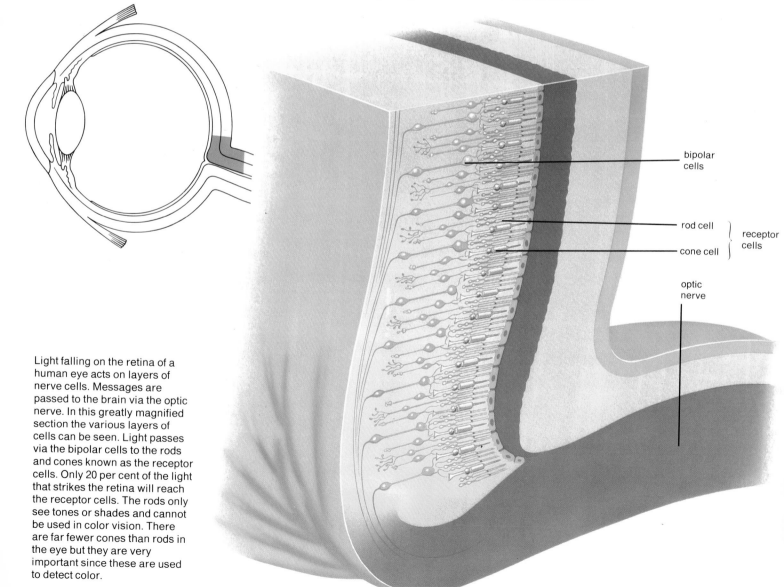

bipolar cells

rod cell ⎫
⎬ receptor cells
cone cell ⎭

optic nerve

Light falling on the retina of a human eye acts on layers of nerve cells. Messages are passed to the brain via the optic nerve. In this greatly magnified section the various layers of cells can be seen. Light passes via the bipolar cells to the rods and cones known as the receptor cells. Only 20 per cent of the light that strikes the retina will reach the receptor cells. The rods only see tones or shades and cannot be used in color vision. There are far fewer cones than rods in the eye but they are very important since these are used to detect color.

only the rods work in poor light and they produce pictures in shades of grey, rather like a black and white photograph.

Scientists think that our ability to see in color is due to there being three types of cone. Each type contains a pigment which is sensitive to one color only, either red, green or blue. These colors are called the **primary colors.** By mixing red, green or blue light we can make any other color. Thus light from a green field would only affect cones with green pigment. Light reflecting off a banana would affect two types of cone, those with green and those with red sensitive pigment. This is because yellow light can be made by mixing green and red lights. When a colored beam of light hits the retina, the three types of cone will break down the light into the three primary colors. By joining together all the messages from cones the brain tells us what color we are seeing.

On the retina of each eye there is a special area called the **fovea** or yellow spot. This is only a millimetre or so across but contains only cones and is very important to our vision. Our clearest color pictures are produced from this part of the retina, tiny though it is. When we look at details in a picture what we really do is move our eyes until the detail is focused on our fovea.

Just how the brain 'sees' a colored picture is still a mystery. However, it helps if we think of vision in the following way. Each cone in the retina deals with one small part of the picture. There are millions of cones in the retina and the brain would be overworked if all sent separate signals. Instead, small groups of cones send their messages to a special nerve cell called a

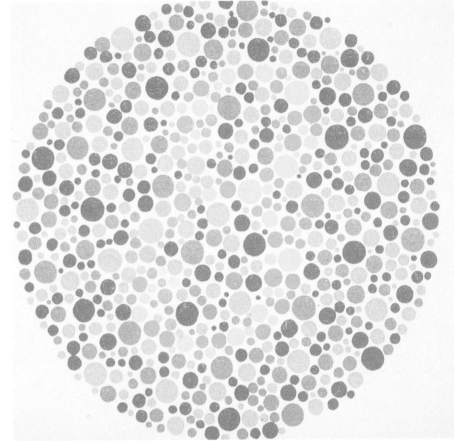

A color blindness detection chart. When checking for color blindness, a series of these charts are used to determine which colors can be seen by the patient. A color blind person would not easily spot the figure 8 in this diagram.

A photograph of the interior of a healthy human eye taken with an ophthalmoscope.

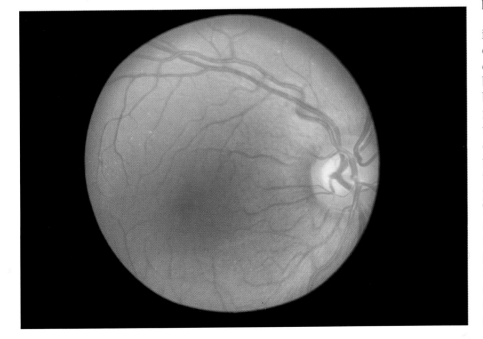

bipolar cell. The job of these bipolar cells is to collect signals from a group of cones and pass them to the brain along a single nerve. The brain then builds up a picture from these signals. We can think of this as a jigsaw puzzle with each piece being a group of cones on the retina. The bipolar cell will receive signals from only one piece. The brain then puts all the pieces back together again to make a complete picture.

When something goes wrong with the cones in our eyes it produces **color blindness.** Eight out of every one hundred men and one out of every one hundred women cannot tell the difference between red, green and grey. This is probably because they do not have the correct cone pigments. In everyday life color-blind people learn to tell the difference between colors of familiar objects such as traffic lights. For instance, the top light of the traffic signal means stop. People to whom color is important, such as airline pilots and police, are given color blindness tests. These are usually cards showing patterns of colored dots. To the person with normal color vision the dots form a shape or a letter. For example, a red-green color-blind person would not see a red figure 8 on a page of green dots. In our lives color is very important in things such as road markings and gardening and in hobbies such as stamp collecting.

Color vision in the living world

IF YOU WATCHED a bee flying around a garden in the summer you would not be at all surprised to see it land on a flower. You may notice that the bee will visit only certain kinds of flowers. Other flowers which look similar to our eyes will not be visited by the bee. The reason why the bee only visits certain flowers is that it can see **ultraviolet** light, which we cannot see. If we took a photograph of the flowers visited, using ultraviolet light, we would see a pattern of dark markings on the petals. These act like the lights on an airport runway and guide the bee towards the nectar in the flower. This is an example of how we must always remember that other animals may not see the world as we do.

The ultraviolet light that bees can see and we cannot is part of the spectrum. The word 'spectrum' originally meant something that can be seen. It was used for the 'rainbow' of colors that we get by breaking up white light with a prism. However, we now know that the whole spectrum is far wider than the small part we see as light. All rays in the spectrum travel in just the same way as visible light. Ultraviolet light has a wavelength a bit shorter than ordinary violet which humans can see.

The 'slice' of the spectrum seen by bees is a little further up the scale of wavelengths than the bit we can see. They sense rays with shorter wavelengths. This means that all the colors containing red look different because bees cannot see red. To a bee a 'white' daisy looks greenish-blue.

The bee's view of color was discovered by Karl von Frisch. This scientist is also famous for discovering the waggling dance that 'scout' bees do to tell the others in the hive where they have found food. Von Frisch fed his bees with bowls of sugar-water which he put down on blue paper. After a time they flew to blue paper even if there was no food on it. He found they could choose the blue paper amongst other sheets in different shades of grey. By doing the same experiment with other colors he found out which ones bees can see. The **primary colors** for bees are ultraviolet, yellow and blue.

A honey bee searching for nectar is attracted to some flowers more than others. While we see a yellow flower as attractive for one reason, the bees see it in a very different manner. In these two photographs of the fleabane flower, the one on the far left has been taken in ultraviolet light, and the one on the left in natural, white light. The center of the flower is much darker under ultraviolet and will attract the bee.

The red cloak of the Spanish bullfighter *(opposite)* is more a sign of danger and excitement to us than it is to the bull, which is color-blind. He charges it because the bullfighter flicks and twists it to annoy him.

ultraviolet light   visible light   infrared light

The spectrum, showing the infrared and ultraviolet bands. Bees see very little red light but do see ultraviolet.

A rattlesnake striking at its prey. The rattlesnake has cells sensitive to infrared near its eyes, which can detect a warm, living thing hiding out of sight to normal vision, for example, in shadow or under leaves.

At the other end of our visible spectrum are the **infrared** rays. Their wavelength is too long for us to see them, but we can sense them as heat through cells in our skin. Rattlesnakes are able to 'see' infrared rays. They have two small pits near their eyes that are crowded with cells that feel heat, like the cells in human skin. The snake uses these to sense the direction, size and shape of a warm living thing such as a mouse. Even hidden animals can be 'seen' by the snake. Infrared cameras are sensitive to heat and can take 'pictures' in the dark.

Experiments like the one von Frisch did with bees need to be done to find out what colors other animals can see, but they are very hard to get right. Some animals, especially birds, may have better color vision than humans. However, apes and monkeys seem to see the world in much the same way as we do.

Spanish bull fighters twirl a red cloak in front of the bull to anger it and make it charge. We

now think that the bull is color-blind and charges the cloak because it moves, not because it is red. After all, why should red make the bull angry? Most animals such as cats, dogs, horses and cows are also thought to be 'color-blind'. Their world is seen in shades of grey and pale shades of color. Fish, reptiles and birds that are out and about in the daytime have color vision. A red-breasted male robin will attack other red-breasted males in his breeding area. Male sticklebacks will chase other red-fronted males. The type of experiment carried out by von Frisch would probably show that these all have good color vision. The animals without color vision rely far more on their other senses, like smell and hearing.

The color blue is very important to frogs, probably because danger to a frog comes from the sky. The frog's eye is very sensitive to blue light and will quickly respond to the shape of a bird in the sky. Aphids have a similar sensitivity to greenish-yellow light. This guides the flying aphids when searching for juicy young leaves to land on.

Perspective

DISTANT OBJECTS appear smaller than things that are close to the eye. This is one of the ways in which we can judge distances. You can see why it happens in the picture. The cone of light rays coming from the object becomes narrower as the object moves away from the eye. The size of the picture on the retina of the eye is halved each time the distance is doubled.

You can prove this easily for yourself by holding up your two thumbs. Hold one at arm's length and the other with your elbow bent so that it is at about half the distance from your eye. Move them so that you can see them just overlapping each other. You will find that the thumb further away appears to be about half the size of the nearer one.

This is why, in the illustration of the railway track, the lines seem to be getting closer together (because the gap between them looks smaller) until they appear to meet on the **horizon**. The place where the lines appear to meet is called the **vanishing point**. And yet we know the railway lines are really **parallel**. They never meet. This effect is called **perspective** and the word comes from a Latin word meaning 'to look through'.

However, although our eyes see everything like this, our actual image of the world is different. Hold up your thumbs again at the same distances as before. Move your arms outwards with one arm bent as before. Now look at your thumbs again. They look almost the same size. This is because your brain knows that they are really the same size, and it corrects the image it is given by your eye to match what it knows. The correction is called **size constancy.**

Look across a street at a tall building and then raise your hand in front of it. You will probably be able to block out the whole building from your eye, but this does not fool you into thinking that the building is tiny. It simply tells you it is some distance away.

Size constancy cannot be reproduced by a camera, because it sees what the eye sees before the image is corrected by the brain. For this reason distant objects, even huge towers, often look too small in photographs. An artist painting the same view can enlarge the tower so that the picture correctly shows what he can see in the distance.

Until about six hundred years ago, artists made no attempt to show distance back, or **depth**, in pictures. Everything was shown flat on the surface. They used size to stand for the

Before the rules of perspective were understood, artists made little effort to create illusions of space in their paintings. This wall painting *(right)* from Thebes, Egypt, dates from 1400BC, and shows a total lack of perspective.

The further an object is from the eye, the smaller is its image on the retina. In this diagram light rays from two identical objects are seen entering the eye.

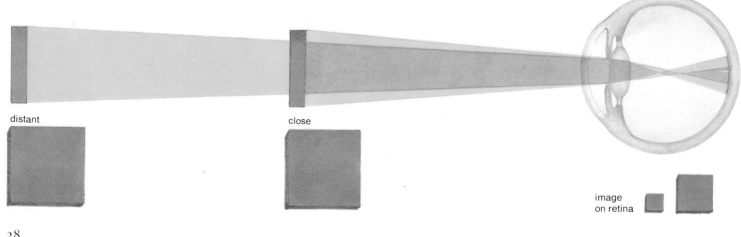

distant

close

image
on retina

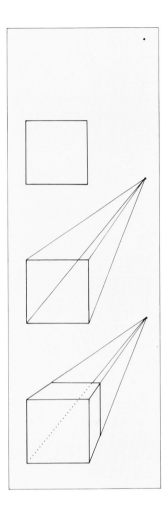

Three stages in how to draw a box. Start by drawing a square. Then choose a vanishing point, and rule lines in pencil to it from the four corners of the square. Now draw two more lines behind the square as shown in the diagram. Finally rub out the lines to the vanishing point beyond and you will be left with a convincing illusion. Try varying the position of the vanishing point; the effect you will get is to see the box from different angles.

importance. A king was painted very large and servants very small.

The artists of the early **Renaissance** in Italy worked out a set of geometrical rules for drawing perspective, and this changed painting completely. It was described by Leonardo da Vinci in his Notebooks. You can see in the painting by Crivelli how it works. The background has depth, and you can compare it with the illustration of the railway. The roofs and ledges of the buildings lead your eye back to a vanishing point, just like the railway track.

Perspective is most easily seen in the buildings of Renaissance paintings, but the artists used the same method for drawing people, animals and objects. They shortened and angled the lines running away from the eye towards a vanishing point (there may be many of these in the same picture). This is called **foreshortening**. It means that things painted on a flat surface appear round and solid, as they do in a photograph.

The Annunciation by Crivelli (*c*1430–95). This picture relies almost entirely on the rules of perspective to create an illusion of three dimensions. It was painted shortly after the discovery of perspective in Italy during the Renaissance period. The artist has used exactly the same rules as apply to the drawing of the box. See if you can work out where the vanishing point is.

The rules of perspective allow the artist to paint the exact image that appears on the retina of the eye. But we know that the brain adjusts this image. Leonardo da Vinci realized that geometry is not all the artist needs to paint the world as it is seen. Other tricks can be used to give an illusion of space and depth in a flat painting. Distant views are usually hazy and their colors are less bright than in the foreground. Shadows help to show the shapes of things. Perspective is a 'tool', like these, which the artist can use as much as he or she wishes.

Perception and optical illusion

WHEN YOU LOOK at an everyday object, such as a cup, you recognize it because you have seen it, or others like it, before. You have learned the shape and can imagine that it is hard and smooth. Even if it is upside down, or has an unusual shape, you will be able to use your imagination to compare it with other cups you remember. You will be able to work out how to use it.

and we come to expect that our perceptions will be right.

Look at the figure below. You can see that it is made up of patches of black and white, but can you perceive the larger shape in the picture? If you can, you are filling in the information missing from the picture from your own experience. If you cannot, you need more information. Read the caption and look again. If you

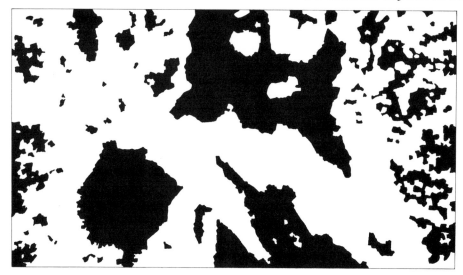

When looking at this picture, you may at first see a patchwork of black and white shapes. However, look carefully at it again and you will see a picture of a man. If you still cannot see the man, turn the book upside down and look at the small illustration below.

The combination of seeing with memory and imagination is called **perception.** It means understanding the meaning of the images seen by the eye and sent to the brain. It would be hard to survive if you could not perceive anything. For instance if you saw a car speeding towards you but had not learned to move out of its way you would probably be run over.

We use sight, like our other senses, to help us to understand the world, and we have to learn how to do this. Newborn babies can see and hear and touch and smell. It may be a few months before they begin to learn how these sensations go together and what they mean.

When a baby is about five months old it has learned that when it sees its mother it will also hear and touch her, and be fed and cuddled. It begins to put together the way things look and the way they feel or taste. The next stage (at about one year old) is to learn that the same object may look different from different angles. Then the baby learns to recognize objects from different distances. As we grow older we continue to learn more about the way things look,

know what to expect you will probably see it. Expectation helps the brain to make sense of the information sent from the eyes, but it can also be disturbing if the information is not as plain as it seems.

The optical **illusions** shown here work because of the difference between our habits of perception and what is actually printed on the page. You can test the lines and circles with a ruler to make sure they are straight and equal in size, but remove the ruler and the illusions will appear again. Even if you know they are tricks you cannot stop yourself being fooled.

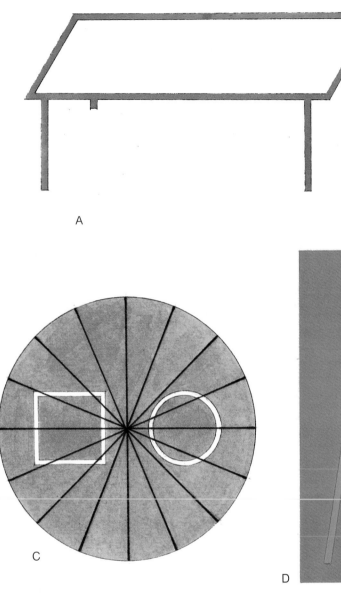

A

B

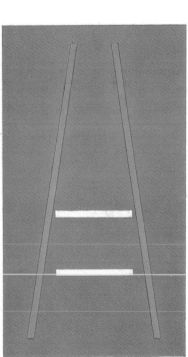

D

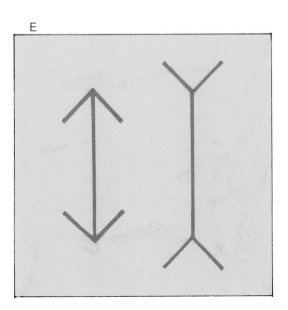

E

F

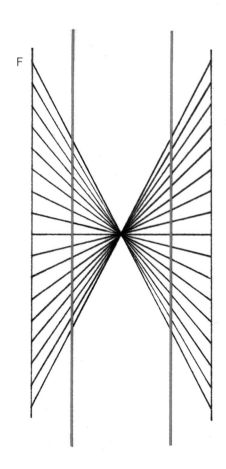

Six well known optical illusions. With all of them, what we think we see is not what is actually there. (A) The *lack* of perspective makes the 'table top' look distorted. Cover the legs and the top now looks a regular shape. (B) Those wavy lines are in fact straight and parallel; you can check with a ruler. (C) The square and the circle in this case do not look square and circular. (D) Because we think the two blue lines are disappearing into the distance we see the two white lines as being different sizes; they are not. (E) Anyone can see that the line on the left is shorter than the one on the right. Check with the ruler again. (F) The red lines bend in the middle; again the eye has been tricked.

Display and camouflage

IMAGINE TRYING to mix the right colors to paint a picture of a peacock. Or, if you had never seen a peacock's tail, do you think you could have invented its pattern? Color and design are very important to us, particularly in the way we dress and decorate our homes. However, human beings are unable to match the beauty and variety of the colors in nature.

The colors of animals and plants are usually there for a purpose. The colored and shimmering tail feathers of the peacock are there to attract the female, the peahen, to mate. Birds have well developed color vision, and the males of many species put on colorful **displays** during the mating season. Plants often have brightly colored flowers to attract insects. By carrying pollen from one flower to the next, the insects help the plants to produce seeds.

Some animals use bright colors as a warning to others. The colors indicate that if they are attacked they will bite, sting or perhaps taste unpleasant. Some South American tree frogs have very poisonous skins. These have colored bands and these act as a warning to predatory animals. The yellow and black stripes of wasps make them easy to recognize and birds soon learn that they will be stung if they attack an insect with these warning stripes. Certain types of poisonous snakes are also brightly colored to give warning that they are dangerous.

However, not all brightly colored animals are poisonous. Some flies which are really quite harmless have **evolved** to look like wasps. In North America the spice-bush swallowtail butterfly (which is harmless) has wings colored to match those of the poisonous pipe-vine swallowtail. This is called **mimicry**. Scientists think that animals which mimic other poisonous types are better protected from predators. The predators learn not to attack the harmless mimics because they look harmful or poisonous. The bright colors of harmful and mimic animals are sometimes called warning colors. Even though these animals are easy to see they are likely to be left alone by predators.

Another way of surviving is by not being seen at all. Animals which use **camouflage** are colored and patterned to match the leaves, soil or rocks on which they live. Camouflage usually works best when the animal keeps still. These species often rest during the day and

The red-eyed tree frog of Central America has bright colors as a warning to others.

The courtship display of the peacock is one of nature's most glorious sights.

move around after dark. Animals such as leopards and tigers, which live in forests, have patterned coats that make them hard to detect in the dappled sunlight. This helps them to hunt without being seen. Young deer are often spotted to help them stay hidden in woodland.

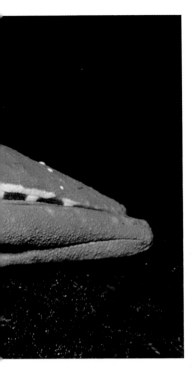

The peppered moth has pale grey wings speckled with black. When it rests on tree trunks covered with grey lichen it is almost invisible to birds. A few types have dark wings and are usually seen and eaten. However, in industrial areas the lichen is killed by air **pollution.** Here the dark moths have become much more common, because they are well camouflaged on dark tree bark. Predatory birds cannot see them easily and this helps them to survive.

As light usually comes from overhead, the undersides of animals are normally in shadow. To avoid this giving away their presence, many species are paler underneath. This coloring is called **countershading.** Nearly all fish, apart from the ones that swim along the seabed, are dark above and silvery below. Their silver scales also reflect light, and make the fish harder to see from below.

While most species hide because they live on a background which matches their own color-ing, a few change the color of their skin instead. Chameleons can become greener, browner, darker or lighter very quickly. In the sea, a shrimp called the chameleon shrimp is even better at this, and can make itself blue, brown, red or green. The octopus is also able to change color quickly to match its background.

Several birds and mammals living in very cold regions become white in winter. The arctic fox, the stoat, and some types of hare, molt their brown fur as the days shorten and grow new white coats for the winter. The ptarmigan and the willow grouse, normally brown birds, sprout white feathers to help them hide in the snow.

Every living thing has its own particular place in nature. Biologists call this its **niche.** This means not only where it lives, but how it fits in with other species, what it eats, and what eats it. The colors and patterns of each species have developed to help it survive in its own niche.

Two varieties of peppered moth. The black form of this moth has become common in industrial areas where lichens are absent from tree trunks due to pollution of the atmosphere.

The Mountain Hare. Like some other mammals and birds that live in cold climates, it grows a new white coat for winter camouflage.

The primary colors

It is important to understand the difference between color in light and color in paint. When white light is passed through a prism, it is split up and we can see all the colors of the visible spectrum. These pure colors can be seen in a rainbow.

Now think of a box of paints or a set of crayons. We see a range of colors, but these colors are not made by splitting white light. You can only change white paint by mixing another color with it. With paint, each color is made from a **pigment**, or from a mixture of pigments. Pigments are colored powders formed by grinding up a wide variety of materials such as different types of earth, rocks, plants or even dead insects. All these things have a natural color, but the colors of pigments are not as pure as the colors of the spectrum.

When light falls on an object, part of the visible spectrum is **absorbed**, or taken in by the object and part is reflected. The parts that are

The colors of the spectrum as seen in a rainbow over a fjord in Norway.

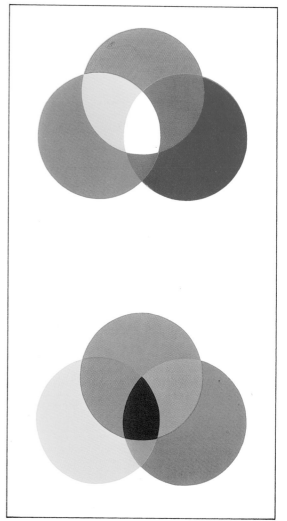

The white, colorless light from the Sun or from the white-hot filament in an electric light bulb is made up of the colors of the spectrum. The three colors – red, green and blue – are known as the primary colors of light. Mixed together they make 'white' light. The secondary colors are magenta, (bluish red), cyan (bluish green) and yellow.

The three primary colors of paint are red, blue and yellow. You can make practically any color you want using just these three colors. When you mix these three colors in exactly the right amounts you get black, not white.

reflected combine to form the colors that our eyes see.

You may wonder how we are able to see some things as black or white. If an object absorbs all the colors of the spectrum, no light is reflected and we see black. If all the colors are reflected, there is no change to the white light, so we see the object as white.

White light contains all the colors of the spectrum, but in fact it can be made by mixing up just three, that are widely spaced across the range of colors. The picture shows the result of shining three beams of light on to a screen, one through a red **filter**, one through a blue filter and one through a green filter. Where all three colors on the screen overlap we get white light. Red, blue and green are called the primary colors. By mixing these three in different amounts we can get any color of the spectrum. Filters are clear glass or plastic sheets that are colored. Only rays the same color as the filter can pass through.

We see colors because of special cells in our eyes called cones. There are three kinds of cone and each kind responds to one of the three primary colors. Our brain senses the whole range of colors by mixing the signals coming from each type of cone.

By mixing red and green light we get yellow. You only need to add the correct amount of blue to yellow and the result is white light. We call blue and yellow **complementary** colors, because we get white light by adding them together.

As you see in the picture blue is opposite to yellow. These are complementary. The complementary color of green is a color called **magenta**. It is a bluish red. The complementary color of red is a bluish green, which we call **cyan.**

If you mix each of the pairs of complementary colors the result will in each case be white light.

Newton's color disk is divided into sections. Each is painted with a color of the spectrum. If very good-quality paints are used it gives the effect of white light when spun very quickly.

Blue, pink and green spotlights when mixed together give a white light, as shown in this cabaret scene.

The reason for this is that all the primary colors are reflected by each pair of complementary colors.

In painting, the mixing of colors is different. As you probably know, mixing blue and yellow paints makes green. Blue paint appears blue because the pigments in it reflect blue light. The colors either side of blue in the spectrum are also reflected a little. These are green and indigo. This is because the pigments are not pure colors. Yellow reflects a little red and green as well as yellow. Yellow paint mixed with blue paint gives a green color because green is the only color reflected by both paints.

With paints, you will have found out that you can make most of the colors you need by mixing blue, yellow and red. These colors are called the primary colors of paint. When you mix red, blue and yellow of exactly the right shades and brightness you get black. In fact, you are more likely to get a dark greyish brown color, as the pigments used in paints are not pure.

Colored filters are often used over white spotlights to light the stage of a theatre. Plain white artificial light can make the actors and sets look dull and cold. Instead, some of the spotlights are covered by pink filters, some by light green and some by light blue. The colors mix together on the stage to give white light. However, the effect is brighter and more like real daylight. Extra pink and yellow filters make the stage look as though the sun is shining. If the scene takes place at night a lot of blue and green filters will be used. Over one hundred different colored filters are used for stage lighting in some of the bigger theaters.

Light sensitivity

WE LIVE in a world of light. Natural light comes from the Sun, moon and stars. By far the most important light is sunlight. The sunlight provides us with a mixture of colors, or types of light, including infrared and ultraviolet rays which we cannot see. All types of light contain **energy**. The energy of infrared rays are obvious to us as heat. If a piece of paper is held close to the fire it will **absorb** the heat and eventually burst into flame.

The ultraviolet part of sunlight contains much more energy than the infrared but does not make things burst into flame. Instead, this type of light breaks down the 'cement', or **bonds**, between the basic building blocks of substances called **molecules**. The effect of ultraviolet light is easily seen if you look at an old piece of net curtain which has been hanging in a window for a long time. New netting is strong and cannot be torn easily. The netting that has hung in a sunny window for a few years gradually falls to pieces. The ultraviolet rays have caused the molecules in the nylon to become 'unstuck'. The bonds between them have broken and the molecules have begun to separate.

Our bodies are made from molecules, and ultraviolet rays can have a similar effect on us, causing the cells to die. In very sunny weather our **exposed** skin becomes darker as we develop a suntan. This is the way our body protects its tissues from ultraviolet rays. The suntan is produced by a colored chemical, or **pigment**, in the skin called **melanin**. This and other chemicals like it are able to soak up, or absorb, the harmful ultraviolet rays and therefore protect the skin.

A very similar process is the basis of photography. A range of chemicals, including **silver bromide**, are very sensitive to most types of light. They start as clear crystals which turn black when light is shone on them. What is happening is that the silver bromide, also called a silver salt, is 'burnt' by the light to leave silver metal. When we take a photograph, we are letting different strengths of light fall on to a layer of silver salts on the film. The production of the final photograph involves using chemicals to **develop** the image and then print it on to a piece of special paper.

This reconstruction shows that taking a picture in Victorian times was a clumsy and long procedure. Often a photographer needed an assistant to help carry equipment. The tripod was a necessity to keep the camera still during the long exposures.

The Frenchman Louis Daguerre (1757–1851) first became famous for the Diorama, a stage lighting device. In 1829 he teamed up with Joseph Niepce, who had successfully produced an image on a metal plate in 1826, after an eight hour exposure. Daguerre's invention, the daguerreotype *(right)* was much quicker, and produced a sharper image. It did not come about until after Niepce's death in 1833.

In the earliest photography, the thin layers of light-sensitive silver salts were spread on to glass plates. The simplest type of early camera was a hollow box which was completely dark inside and had a tiny pinhole in one side. Opposite the pinhole was placed a frosted glass screen so that the photographer could see the picture. To take a photograph this screen was replaced by a glass photographic **plate**. This had to be done in the dark to prevent light from ruining the specially prepared plate.

The pinhole acted like a very simple lens and produced a clear inverted image at the back of the camera box. This image was very faint because only a little light came through the pinhole. An early photographer used to look through the back of the camera under a black cloth to keep the screen in the dark. Another problem was that the plate had to be left exposed for a long time for an image to appear. Some early cameras needed up to eight hours to produce a picture. This was partly overcome by the use of a glass lens which let in much more light and produced sharp pictures. Even then it often took several minutes to produce a good photograph on glass.

In 1839 a Frenchman, Louis Daguerre, invented a process known as daguerreotype. He used a silvered-copper plate instead of glass. After exposure of several minutes in a camera the image on the plate was developed with the use of a chemical vapor. The plate was then 'fixed', making the image permanent. By 1840 the process became widely used and as the exposure time had been reduced to one minute, it became possible to take portraits.

Meanwhile, an English photographer, William Fox Talbot, had found out how to make paper prints. He prepared sensitive paper by treating it with a solution of common salt, then washing it with a solution of silver nitrate. The paper darkened rapidly when exposed to light. Fox Talbot's discoveries, including the paper print, are the basis of modern photography. In 1888 George Eastman introduced the Kodak camera, and photography soon became widely used throughout the world.

An early French camera, the Dubroni Collodion, 1864. The earliest cameras were simply light-tight boxes with a lens at the front. The light-sensitive plate was placed in the rear of the box; it was exposed by removing the lens cap for a period up to several minutes. Then the chemicals were carefully introduced to process the plate and fix the image.

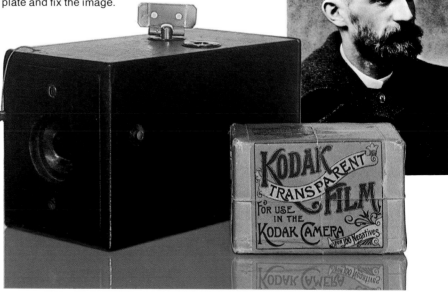

George Eastman (right), famous for producing the first Kodak camera in 1888. This system was the first to use roll film (as opposed to plates) and was both quicker and less complicated to use than earlier cameras. In 1895 he introduced the first Brownie camera, which quickly became popular with amateur photographers.

How a camera works

IN MANY WAYS a camera is very similar to the human eye. Both have a lens to collect all the light rays from a scene and form a sharp, clear picture or image. They both control the amount of light that goes into the image. The main difference between the eye and the camera is that the eye passes the image on to our brain and the camera records the image on film. In our brain the image is not always 'seen' exactly as it appears. The brain can add pieces of information to what the eye sees whereas a camera records the image exactly. Yet another difference between the eye and the camera is that the eye is only sensitive to visible light. Some cameras can record types of 'light' that are invisible to us, such as infrared and ultraviolet.

The lens of the camera is contained in a tube called a lens body. It is a carefully shaped piece of glass that 'bends' the light rays to form a clear picture on the film. The sharpness, or **focus**, of this picture is controlled by moving the lens nearer to or further away from the film. There are many different kinds of lens. The main ones are called **wide-angle, standard** and **telephoto** lenses. The picture produced by a wide-angle lens includes much more of a scene than we can see by simply looking ahead. The standard lens, usually fitted to the camera when you first buy it, produces a picture covering the same view as you can see looking straight ahead. The telephoto lens works like a telescope, making things seem nearer and larger. If we used a wide-angle lens in an ordinary room we would take a picture of a large part of the room at once. From the same place in the room a picture taken with the telephoto lens would only include a part of the opposite wall, but the image would be magnified.

A range of camera lenses. The lens is the key part of any camera. The degree of refraction, or bending, of light, depends on their shape. The more curved a lens is, the greater, or wider, is the angle of view. Because it is curved, the light focuses at a shorter distance than through a flatter lens. This distance is known as 'focal length'. The flatter the lens is, the less is the angle of view, and the longer is the focal length; this results in a magnified image and the lens is known as a telephoto. In the picture, the taller lenses are telephoto and the shortest are wider angled.

There are many other types of special lens, including the 'fish-eye' lens, which gives the widest possible picture. A fairly recent invention has been the **zoom lens**, which has many small glass lenses inside the one body. This can be altered to telephoto by moving a tube on the outside of the lens body.

Inside the lens body is a small piece of metal that can be opened up or closed down to change the size of a hole or **aperture** through which light has to pass. This aperture is called the **iris diaphragm** and it can be compared to the iris in the human eye. The aperture is controlled by a ring around the lens body called the aperture ring. The iris diaphragm controls the amount of light that reaches the film. The ring that alters the size of the aperture in the iris diaphragm is marked at regular intervals with numbers such as 2, 2.8, 4, 5.6, 8, 11, 16 and 22. These are called **f-stops**. The higher the number, the smaller the hole or aperture and the less light reaches the film. The amount of light reaching the film is cut down by half when the hole size is changed from one f-stop to the next highest.

The single-lens reflex camera (SLR) allows the photographer to see through the lens by means of a prism and mirror. When the shutter is released the mirror springs up to let the light reach the film. The resulting picture will be exactly as the photographer saw it.

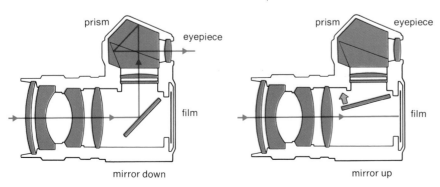

prism

eyepiece

film

mirror down

prism

eyepiece

film

mirror up

As well as affecting the amount of light reaching the film, the size of the aperture also affects how much of the picture is clear, or in focus. If you take a picture of a tree in a park, with the aperture ring set at the f2 stop, the tree will be in focus, but the grass in front and behind the tree will be blurred or out of focus. If you now take the same picture with the aperture ring set at the f16 stop, the tree will still be in focus. However, the grass in front of and behind the tree will also be in focus. This is known as **depth of field**; the higher the f-stop used, the more of your picture will be in focus.

The camera body is a light-proof box which holds the film and further adjusts the amount of light reaching the film. This is done by a metal or fabric 'trap-door' called the **shutter** which opens for a moment to allow light to reach the film. Most cameras have a knob which alters the speed at which the shutter opens. Shutter speeds can vary from 1/2000th of a second to several seconds. Each speed-setting lets in half as much light as the one before. Too much light reaching the film makes the picture look washed-out, too little and it looks dark. To help us get the correct amount of light, many cameras have a built-in **exposure meter.** This contains a special chemical that produces a tiny electrical current when light is shone on it. The more light, the bigger the current. The exposure meter tells us what shutter speed and f-stop to use for any picture we wish to take.

In taking a picture, we use the exposure meter to give the correct setting. Nowadays many cameras do this for you automatically.

The next step is to look through the window, or **viewfinder**, on the back of the camera. This gives you an idea of what will be included in the picture and helps you to focus. The film must then be wound-on, ready to be exposed. The final part, often the most difficult, is to hold the camera very steady, and smoothly squeeze the shutter-release button.

The interior of the Space Shuttle photographed with a very wide-angle, or 'fish-eye' lens. In this confined space the image produced by a standard lens would only include the central section of the scene.

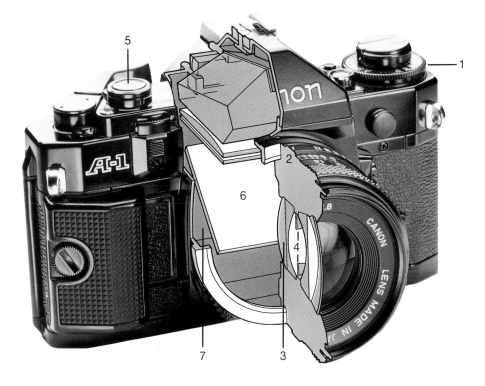

A 35mm single-lens reflex camera. This cutaway diagram shows how complex the internal workings of a modern camera are. Levers, cogs, springs and lenses have to be made with careful precision to give the photographer the best result. Before taking a picture the shutter speed (1) the aperture (2) and the focus have to be chosen. To expose the film, light passes through the lens (3) via the iris diaphragm (4) which controls the aperture. By pressing the shutter release (5) the reflex mirror (6) springs up to allow the light to reach the film (7) after which the film is wound on.

Developing and printing

THE FIRST FILMS were made by George Eastman as early as 1871. These were made from a clear plastic-like material called **celluloid.** This could be rolled into reels and would not tear or break. On to this strong but thin base was spread a very thin layer of a mixture of silver salts and the same substance that makes jelly set, **gelatin.** This mixture is called a photographic **emulsion.** An emulsion is a liquid or jelly in which very fine particles are suspended. The secret of photographic film lies in the minute grains of silver salts which are sensitive to light.

Modern film uses a slightly different base called **cellulose acetate** because it was found that celluloid used to catch fire very easily. Another difference is that the base is now colored bluish-grey to prevent light reflecting off the base, back into the emulsion. By altering the mixture of silver salts in the emulsion, we can affect the amount of light needed to produce a picture. This is known as **film speed** and is given a number which is printed on the film carton. So called 'fast' films are very sensitive to light and are used on dull days or indoors. The 'slow' films need much more light but give a more detailed picture. Almost all film is produced as rolls, either inside a can or sealed in a plastic cassette. A new type of film is the **disk-film.** This has tiny pieces of film set around a plastic disk. The important rule with all types of film is to keep it cool and in the dark until it has been exposed and developed.

An image or picture is produced on film by light turning tiny crystals of silver salts into metallic silver. No metal will let light pass through, it is **opaque**, and the minute grains of silver on the film appear dark because of this. Parts of the picture that were white reflect lots of light and appear on the **developed** film as black areas. Parts of the picture that were black do not reflect much light and appear as pale or clear patches on the film. The developed film is called a **negative** because the bits that should be white are black and vice versa. A negative of this page would have black paper and white lettering.

If we could examine the film in the camera before and after exposure we would notice no change in appearance. When light strikes the film, the silver salts are broken down but the image is hidden. To reveal the images on the film it has to be treated with chemicals, or developed. After the film has been used, it is taken out of the camera in the dark and placed in a light-proof container called a developing tank. Once safely in the tank, solutions of chemicals can be poured in and out. The first part of development involves a chemical called a **developer.** This actually changes the hidden image on the film into a real one of silver grains and unexposed silver salts. This process takes around five minutes at room temperature for most black and white films.

Now the film shows a copy of the original picture with blacks and whites reversed. To make this image stay, or remain permanent, we use a chemical called a **fixer.** This washes out all the unexposed silver salts and stops the negative fading after a time. The final part of producing the negative is to wash it for a long time in water to get rid of all the chemicals.

Obviously, an exact opposite of our picture, in terms of black and white, is not much use to us. We have to use the negative to make a **positive.** To do this, we work in a dark room where the negative is placed in an **enlarger** which is really the opposite of a camera. The enlarger has a powerful light inside which is shone through the negative and focused by a lens to form an image on a piece of paper. This paper is called photographic paper and is coated with emulsion in the same way as film. Once the image from the negative has been focused, the light in the enlarger is switched off. A piece of photo-

There are numerous types of film available today to suit a wide range of camera designs. When choosing a film it is as well to have an idea of the lighting conditions and the subject to be photographed. Film speeds vary from very slow, for example ASA 25, to very fast, for example ASA 1000. (ASA stands for American Standards Association.) A slow film is only suitable in good lighting conditions. Its advantage is that it gives a very much sharper image than a fast film. In poor lighting conditions a fast film is needed; this tends to give a grainy effect to the image.

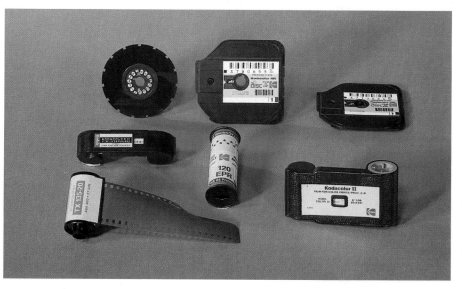

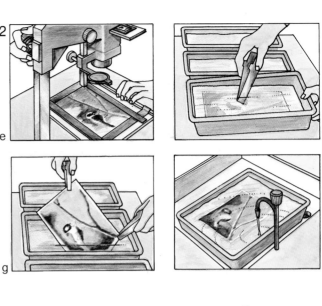

1

Processing a black-and-white film. In complete darkness the film is wound on to a reel and then placed into a developing tank (a). Chemicals are then added in two stages, firstly to develop the film and secondly to fix the image (b, c), after which the film is rinsed thoroughly (d).

2

Once the film is dried it is ready for printing in the darkroom. The negative is placed in the enlarger, and the image exposed on to photographic paper (e). The paper is then placed into a developing tray for about one and a half minutes (f). It is then rinsed and placed in the fixing tray for ten to twenty minutes (g). Finally a thorough wash removes all traces of chemicals (h) before the print is dried.

Processing times are very important to obtain good results. All dark rooms should have an accurate timer.

graphic paper is now placed under the enlarger and the enlarger's light is switched on again for a few seconds. After this the paper is developed in open dishes, still in the darkroom. Unlike the emulsion on films, that of photographic paper is not affected by red light. This means that the whole process can be done under a very dull red light called a safety-light.

Producing photographs in color is much more complicated. Color film has three layers of emulsion. One layer records blue; one records red; and the other layer records green light. Developing these films is very difficult and it is usually done in special film laboratories. The paper on which color negatives are printed also has three layers of emulsion but must be handled in the dark as it is sensitive to all colors of light.

A darkroom is the photographer's laboratory. It needs to be well planned, light-tight and ventilated since fumes from the chemicals can be dangerous. This picture shows a complex color enlarger being used.

Motion pictures

THE MOVING PICTURE, or **cinematograph**, is possible only because of a special feature of the human eye. If we are shown a picture, or image, we continue to 'see' that image for one-tenth of a second after it has been taken away. In motion pictures the moving object is broken down into a series of still pictures. Each of these pictures can be understood by our eye and providing they are shown to us at more than ten per second, we cannot tell the difference between them and real movement. As we still have the image of the previous picture in our mind when the next one appears, our brain simply blends them all together as one smooth motion.

The first 'moving pictures' were produced as long ago as 1833. This was done by joining together the ends of a strip of cardboard to form a cylinder. Inside the cylinder were drawn figures in various stages of movement. Opposite each drawing was a slot in the cardboard through which a picture could be seen. By spinning the cylinder around a central shaft and looking through the slots, an illusion of movement was created. This was called a **zoetrope** and became a popular nineteenth century toy.

The early movie cameras were hand-cranked, heavy objects that were mounted on tripods to keep them still. The normal speed was only 16 frames per second as opposed to 24 frames per second in later cameras. Films taken on these early cameras appear jumpy when compared with modern movies.

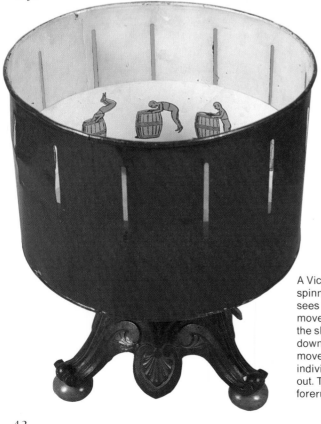

A Victorian zoetrope. By spinning the cylinder, the eye sees an illusion of continuous movement when looking through the slots. As the cylinder slows down, the eye sees a flicker of movement, and finally the individual pictures can be made out. The zoetrope was the forerunner of the movie age.

We measure the number of pictures seen in one second as **frames** per second. This name comes from the appearance of movie film. The very early films were a bit slower than modern movies and were jerky. You can create a similar effect by blinking two or three times per second while watching something moving. This gives a jerky picture as you miss parts of the movement. Present day 'home movies' use sixteen frames per second and the better-quality films use twenty-four frames per second.

The movie camera works in a similar way to the ordinary camera. The main difference is that it has to take up to twenty-four tiny pictures every second. Each one of these individual frames has to stay perfectly still while the image is shone on the film. This is done using a specially shaped wheel that pulls the film into position behind the lens, then lets go for a fraction of a second. Once the film has stopped moving, a **shutter** opens between the film and lens, and light reaches the film. As the shaped wheel comes around once more, to move on the film, the shutter is closed and the next frame is positioned behind the lens. Thus the film moves through the camera in a series of jerks. Unlike ordinary film, the movie film comes in long reels up to 30 m long. The long lengths are needed because even at the slower speed of sixteen frames per second. 30 m will last only for ten minutes. Imagine how many feet of film are needed for each full length film you see at the movies. To help the photographer, the movie camera has a dial on the side which tells him how much film has been used.

Movie film comes in three main types depending upon the width of the film. The smallest size, used by most home movie makers, is called 8 mm. The next size is 16 mm and is used for many films that you see on the television. The 'big screen' pictures shown at your local movie theater are taken on 35 mm film. This larger size gives a much better quality picture and allows plenty of room to add a sound recording.

All films are shown on a machine called a **projector**. It has been given this name because it throws, or projects, the image on to a white wall, or screen. The projector works by shining a very powerful light through the film and uses a lens to focus the image on the screen. The film is moved forward through the projector in a series of jumps, as in the camera, stopping only to allow a shutter to open. The shutter in the projector opens to let the powerful beam of light shine through the film. It is important that the film is moved through the projector at the same speed as it was taken, otherwise movements would be speeded up or slowed down. The very bright light is produced by an electric bulb. This can get very hot and has to be cooled by the flow of air from a fan.

The screen is a very important part of a movie theater. The image from the projector, although bright when seen in a dark room, is quite weak. To get the brightest picture, the screen needs to reflect as much light as possible. One way of helping a screen to reflect more light is to cover it with small glass beads that have been split in half. Many of the better-quality movie screens are treated in this way.

Motion cameras follow the same principle, whether amateur or professional (as below). The more complex professional camera, however, has better quality, changeable lenses, and uses a larger-sized film. Some types of film include a sound track, but in this case the sound would be recorded separately on a tape recorder. Note here the number of lenses, and the bellows which prevent any unwanted reflections when filming.

A eyepiece; B film; C film gate; D lens; E alternative lenses; F bellows.

A home-movie projector (right) uses an electric motor for its drive. The film travels from the front spool via a system of cogs. It passes between the lamp and the lens and then on to the take-up spool at a constant rate. The powerful projector bulb soon gets hot and has to be cooled by a fan.

A lamp; B projector lens; C film gate; D cooling fan.

High-speed and time lapse photography

OUR EYES AND BRAIN work in such a way that some things appear to move in a 'blur' and others seem motionless. To see movement clearly, the brain must be able to recognize separate pictures, or images, that are gradually changing. By using movie film, we can break down movement, fast or slow, into individual images that the brain can understand.

In an ordinary movie camera, the film stops behind the lens twenty-four times per second, that is twenty-four frames per second. Each time the film stops, a shutter opens and allows light coming through the lens to form the image on the film. This basic way of producing pictures on movie film can be used by special cameras at up to five hundred frames per second. Above this speed it is mechanically impossible to keep stopping and starting the film for each picture.

Very quick movements are recorded by high-speed cameras. These take up to 11,000 pictures, or frames, per second. To produce single pictures as quickly as 11,000 times per second we use a continuously moving film. Normally, there would not be enough light to expose this rapidly moving film. One way of producing single images on the film is to use a very rapidly flickering light called a **stroboscope**. This is really a powerful **flash-unit** which produces a very bright flash of light, lasting for only a tiny fraction of a second. Each time the light flashes, a single picture is produced on the film. The repeating flashes of the stroboscope create the effect of 'frames' on the film.

All high-speed films are shown by a projector at the normal speed of twenty-four frames per second. In slowing down the film, something that happened in a fraction of a second can be drawn out into several minutes. Such slowed down action films are very useful to the scientist, who can see just how a cheetah runs or how a fly lands on a ceiling. These films also

Not three moths, but one, photographed at the moment of take-off from a leaf, by multiflash. The flight of insects is something that we take for granted because we see it so often. But flying is hard work for the moth and uses up a great amount of energy. The wings are not moved by muscles, as we might think, but by changes in the shape of the thorax, the center section of the insect's body. The wings flap down as the thorax expands, and lift as it contracts.

provide us with interesting pictures of simple things, such as a raindrop hitting a puddle.

To produce clear photographs of a rapidly moving animal is more difficult than taking a high-speed movie film. The secret is to use an **electronic flash** to light the moving animal or object. The brief, but intense, burst of light produced by these flash units stops any action or movement. Even a small unit can produce a burst of light that lasts a mere 1/400 of a second. Specially built units can reduce this burst of light to 1/25,000 of a second. This is a short enough time to stop any movement and has been used to produce beautiful pictures of insects and birds in a split second of flight.

At the other end of the scale are the movements that are too slow for us to notice. Obvious examples of this are plants growing, flowers opening or our own fingernails growing. Even

A light bulb shattering at the moment of impact.

What happens when a balloon is pricked with a pin. The boy's eyes are closed but the camera's eye is open.

This multiple image of a single raindrop falling into water is something which the human eye is unable to capture.

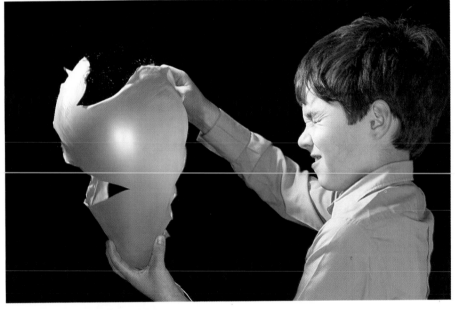

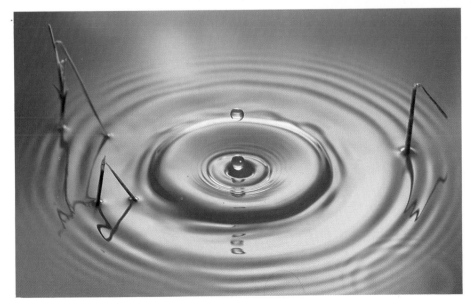

the changing seasons produce 'movement' in the landscape. By using a method called **time lapse** photography, all these actions can be brought together in a few seconds of movie film. This is done by taking a single frame at a time. The slower the movement, the longer the time between taking each frame. A film of a developing flower would be made by taking one frame every five minutes. The change in landscape, as seasons come and go, is best shown by taking one frame every few hours.

A type of time lapse photography has been used for many years to make cartoons. These are films made by drawing thousands of individual pictures, each slightly different from the last. One or two frames of each drawing are filmed to produce the well known moving characters.

The electromagnetic spectrum

ALL MATTER is made of atoms. Each atom consists of a central **nucleus** which has a positive charge. Particles, called **electrons,** move rapidly about it. These are negatively charged. Some materials, such as metals, contain a large number of free electrons, which may wander freely between the atoms. A piece of metal connected across a battery becomes electrically negative at one end, and positive at the other. The free electrons are attracted to the electrically positive end, and move towards it. This movement is called an **electric current.**

At the beginning of the nineteenth century, it was realized that there was a connection between electricity and **magnetism.** In 1820, Oersted showed that a magnet always sets itself at right angles to a wire carrying an electric current. Then Ampère noted that a small loop of wire, with an electric current flowing through it, behaved exactly like a magnet. Magnets have two **poles,** called the north and south magnetic poles. Ampère's current loop also had a north and south pole. The current loop had two sides. Which was north and which was south depended on the direction the electric current flowed round the loop.

In 1831, Michael Faraday found that if a magnet was moved near a piece of wire, then an electric current would flow in the wire. Today, it is believed that the sources of all magnetism are electric currents. You may have placed a bar magnet under a sheet of white paper and sprinkled iron filings over the paper. When you gently tap the paper, the iron filings arrange themselves into a pattern around the bar magnet. This pattern is called a **magnetic field.** The curving lines shown by the pattern of iron filings are called **magnetic lines of force.** In a similar way, an electrically charged body is surrounded by an **electric field.** Two bodies, one with a positive charge and one with a negative charge, are connected by electric lines of force.

In 1846, Faraday suggested that the strengths of the magnetic and electric fields were carried along their lines of force by a wave motion which he called an **electromagnetic wave.** Imagine a long rope fixed at one end. If you hold the other end and shake it up and down, a wave is sent along the rope. In an electric or magnetic field, your rope would be the same as the lines of force. The wave travelling

along them would depend on the strength of the electric or magnetic field.

Faraday's ideas caused the great mathematician James Clerk Maxwell to think about electromagnetic waves. In 1864, he showed that electromagnetic waves were possible. He also showed that they would all travel at a particular speed. To find this speed, some accurate measurements were needed. In 1868, Maxwell made the necessary measurements. He found that electromagnetic waves travelled at about 280,000 km per second. In 1856, two scientists, named Weber and Kohlrausch, had already tried to work out the speed at which electromagnetic waves travel. They used a different method and got a value of about 310,000 km per second.

Around 1850, both Fizeau and Foucault had measured the speed of light, and found this to be about 300,000 km per second. As the speed of electromagnetic waves was roughly equal to the speed of light, Maxwell suggested that light was also an electromagnetic wave. He thought there was a close link between electricity, magnetism and light. We now know that all electromagnetic waves have the same properties as light waves. For example, they can be reflected and refracted, and will travel through the vacuum of outer space.

In 1887, Heinrich Hertz discovered another type of electrical wave. We now call these **radio waves.** An electric charge at rest is surrounded by an unmoving electric field. If the charge is made to vibrate, ripples will form in the electric field and in the magnetic field formed by the

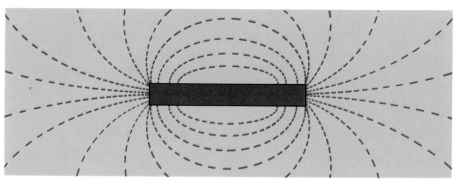

This diagram shows how iron filings would be arranged in a pattern around an ordinary bar magnet, if sprinkled over a piece of paper. The pattern is called a magnetic field and the lines and curves are known as magnetic lines of force. The Earth itself is surrounded by a similar magnetic field stretching out into space.

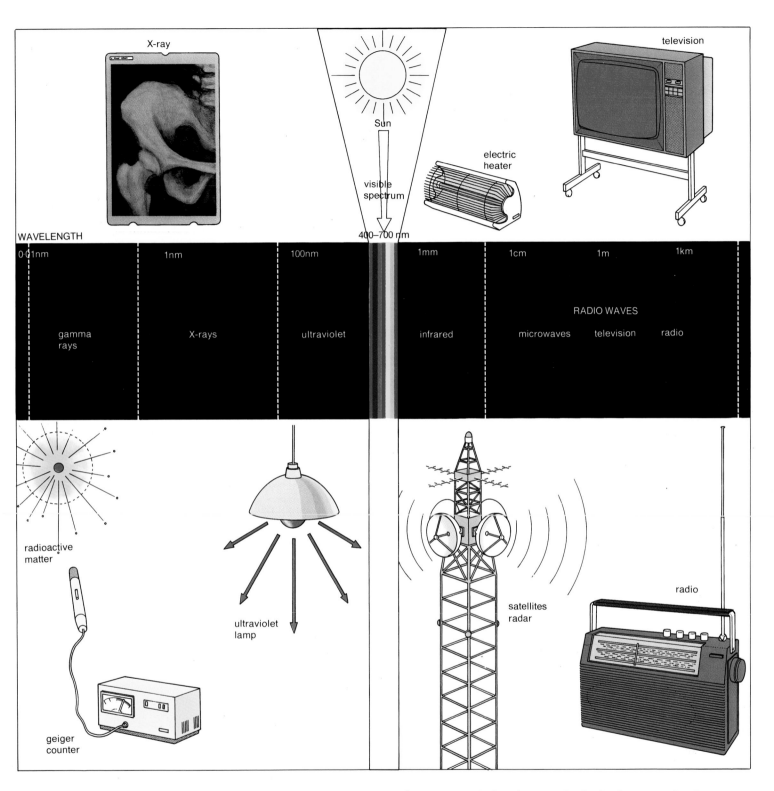

WAVELENGTH

0.01nm	1nm	100nm		1mm	1cm	1m	1km

gamma rays · X-rays · ultraviolet · infrared · RADIO WAVES (microwaves · television · radio)

television

X-ray

Sun

visible spectrum
400–700 nm

electric heater

radioactive matter

geiger counter

ultraviolet lamp

satellites radar

radio

The wavelengths of electro-magnetic radiations are measured in metric units. Some of these wavelengths are very short. The wavelength of X-rays is only one thousand-millionth of a meter. Scientists call this length 1 nanometer, 'nm' for short. The wavelength of gamma rays is even shorter than that of X-rays, 0.01 nm, or one-hundredth of a nanometer.

moving charge. This is the same as dropping a pebble into a pool of water. The waves or ripples move out from where the pebble hit the water to the sides of the pool. The distance between the tops of any two neighboring waves is called the wavelength. The number of times that the waves rise and fall every second is called the frequency.

The wavelength and frequency of an electro-magnetic wave are also related to the speed of

light. If you multiply the frequency by the wave-length for any wave, you obtain the value for the speed of light (that is, 300,000 km per second). There are many different kinds of electromagnetic wave. Sometimes they are called electromagnetic **radiation.** We group all the different types of this radiation together. This grouping is in order of increasing wave-length (decreasing frequency) and is called the electromagnetic spectrum.

47

Beyond red in the spectrum

WE CAN SEE only a very small part of the electromagnetic spectrum. We call this **visible light.** Red light has the longest wavelength in this region, about seven ten-thousandths of a millimeter. This is written as 700 **nanometers** or 700 nm for short. The visible band extends from a wavelength of 380 nm at the violet end, to 780 nm at the red end. However, there is a large part of the electromagnetic spectrum which consists of waves having longer wavelengths (but lower frequency) than red visible light. We cannot see this part of the electromagnetic spectrum.

In 1800, Sir William Herschel carried out some experiments with light. He was interested in the heating power of the various colors of the visible spectrum. He produced a spectrum from white sunlight, and allowed it to fall on to the blackened bulb of a sensitive thermometer. He found that the heating effect increased towards the red end of the spectrum. In fact, it went on increasing beyond the red light which he could see. He had discovered infrared, or IR radiation. This is often divided into four regions, according to its wavelength.

Herschel's experiment showed that IR rays could be refracted by a prism. He also proved that they could be reflected by a polished metal plate, in the same way as visible light waves bounce off a mirror. Most IR radiation is absorbed by glass, but a little of it will pass through. It was this that Herschel detected. The fact that most IR radiation does not pass through glass causes something called the **greenhouse effect.** Imagine a car parked in hot sunshine. The temperature inside may get much higher than the air temperature outside. This is because visible light passes through the glass of the car windows and is absorbed by objects inside the car. These then re-radiate the light at much longer wavelengths as IR radiation. This cannot pass back through the glass, and the car heats up. The same thing occurs inside a glasshouse. The plants absorb the visible light and re-radiate it as IR radiation. This is then trapped inside the greenhouse.

When infrared radiation falls on the skin, it gives a sensation of warmth, and is sometimes called heat or **thermal radiation.** It makes up the greatest part of the radiation given off by the atoms in a hot body. As you heat a substance the atoms at first vibrate to and fro rather slowly, and give off IR waves. As it gets hotter, the atoms vibrate faster and start to give off red visible light. We say the material is red hot. As the temperature rises, more and more visible light of other colors is given off. This mixes to produce white light. We say the material is white hot.

An important use of infrared radiation is in **thermal imaging.** This is where pictures are produced by the IR waves given off by an object,

Inside a steel plant, steel tubing is being worked on under extreme heat. The steel is white-hot near the heat source. It becomes red-hot as it begins to lose heat.

Sir William Herschel was a musician who later became an astronomer. In addition to discovering IR radiation he is best known for his discovery of the planet Uranus in the year 1781.

Light passes through glass into a greenhouse. There it is absorbed by the plants and surfaces, which re-radiate it as IR radiation. Since the wavelength is now longer it cannot pass back through the glass and is trapped as heat inside the greenhouse.

In this IR photograph from space, the colors are not the real colors we would see with the naked eye. They show the amount of radiation given off. Plant life appears red and water appears black or blue.

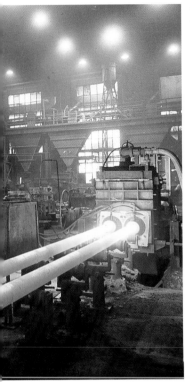

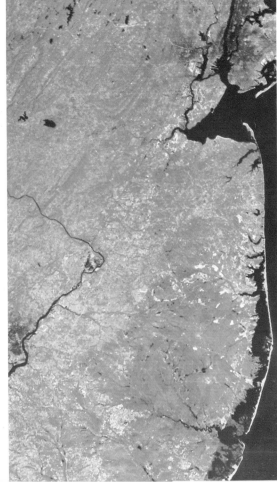

able to find unhealthy parts of the body, called cancer cells, because they emit more heat than normal healthy ones.

Beyond infrared waves we have the microwaves. These have wavelengths between 1 mm and 30 cm. Microwaves are used for communications (particularly in space), as well as in radio astronomy. Much has been learned about bodies in outer space using special telescopes which can pick up microwaves. Microwaves having wavelengths between 1 mm and 1 cm are called millimeter waves.

Radio waves occupy a very wide band of the electromagnetic spectrum beyond the microwaves. They have the longest wavelengths of all, ranging from about 30 cm to many kilometers. These waves are generally given off by electronic circuits. The electricity which you find in your home has a frequency of only about 50 or 60 cycles per second. It radiates an electromagnetic wave with a wavelength of 6000 km. There is no upper limit to the wavelength for radio waves. The higher frequency radio waves are used for television and radio broadcasting.

IR thermal imaging is used in medicine to record changes in the temperature of the body which may indicate injuries or diseases. The color scale usually goes from white (hottest) through yellow, red, purple and green to blue (coldest).

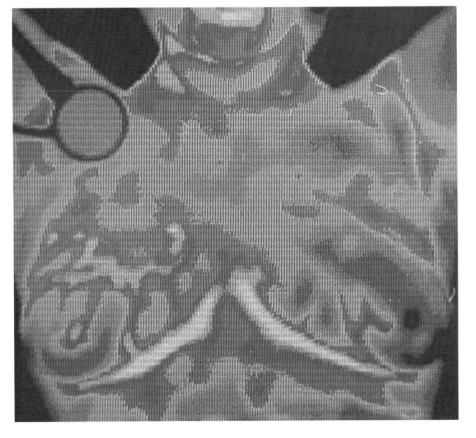

or group of objects. Special photographic films are sensitive to some IR radiation. These enable photography to be carried out in darkness. Although an object in the dark will not be reflecting any visible light, it will give off thermal radiation. There are also special pieces of electronic equipment which can pick up IR waves. It is then possible to convert them into an electrical signal to produce an IR picture on a television screen. Some police forces use devices like this for 'seeing' in the dark.

Infrared pictures are taken of the Earth by satellites orbiting several hundred kilometers above it. Some show the movement of clouds in the atmosphere, and help with the weather reports. They may also show areas of healthy and unhealthy plant growth. A healthy plant normally appears bright red on an IR picture. A plant that is unhealthy will reflect infrared light very differently. Also, clean, clear water appears black, while water which is heavily polluted appears blue. These colors are not the real colors as seen from space. They represent the amount of IR radiation reflected from each object. Infrared photography may be used to take pictures of the human body. Doctors are

Beyond violet in the spectrum

HAVE YOU EVER wondered why the sky appears blue? Let us think about what happens when white sunlight reaches the Earth and enters our atmosphere. Here it is reflected in all directions by millions of tiny particles of dust or water droplets. Another name for this is scattering. Different wavelengths of light are scattered by different amounts. The shortest wavelengths at the blue end of the spectrum are scattered the most. The scattering of blue light is about ten times as great as that for red light. Other colors are scattered less than the blue but more than the red. Because the sky contains such a very large number of tiny particles, the scattered light is easily seen, and the sky appears blue. If it were not for this scattering, a cloudless sky would appear black except towards the Sun.

The deep red color of the Sun as it sinks low in the west at sunset, can also be explained. At this time, the Sun's rays pass through a much thicker layer of atmosphere to reach your eyes than they do at midday. Nearly all of the shorter wavelength blue light from the Sun is scattered out by the tiny particles in this dense layer. So,

far more red light than blue reaches your eyes, and the globe of the setting Sun appears red.

Violet light has the shortest wavelength in the visible spectrum; it is about four ten-thousandths of a millimeter, or 400 nm. A large part of the electromagnetic spectrum consists of waves with shorter wavelengths (but higher frequency) than violet visible light. In 1777, Carl Scheele explored how different colors of the spectrum affected the substance silver chloride. This changes color from white to purple when exposed to sunlight. Scheele found that the change occurred more quickly towards the violet end of the spectrum. In 1801, Johann Ritter discovered invisible rays beyond the violet end of the visible spectrum. These became known as ultraviolet or UV radiation. Shortly afterwards, William Wollaston proved that UV rays made the silver chloride change color very quickly. In 1842, A. E. Becquerel used paper soaked in silver chloride to take crude 'photographs' of the ultraviolet part of the spectrum.

Many early experiments were made difficult because glass is not transparent to UV light. Later, the spectrum was produced by reflection

from a special, very finely ruled grating. Studies of UV radiation were then much easier to carry out. Ultraviolet rays have wavelengths between 380 nm and about 12 nm. The natural source of UV radiation is the Sun. Most UV rays are absorbed high in the atmosphere by a substance called **ozone**. If this did not happen an enormous quantity of UV radiation would reach the ground. This would be extremely dangerous to all forms of life. Sunburn is caused when the small amount of ultraviolet radiation reaching the ground is absorbed by the skin. In small quantities, UV radiation is necessary for the good health of living organisms. Near a large industrial city, the amount of UV light reaching the ground may be nearly zero. This is because the industrial haze above the city absorbs any UV radiation before it reaches the ground.

When UV radiation falls upon certain substances, a process called **fluorescence** may occur. This takes place when atoms of the substance absorb the invisible UV radiation and then re-radiate it at a longer wavelength. This will be visible to the human eye. The color of the fluorescent light depends on the substance, but blue and green are quite common. Sometimes a substance gives off light for many minutes or even hours after the source of UV light has been switched off. This is called **phosphorescence**. The quantity of phosphorescent light

Weak sunlight through industrial haze and smoke-laden atmosphere. Ultraviolet radiation is absorbed before it reaches the ground.

Beyond ultraviolet rays we have the X-rays. These have wavelengths from about 12 nm down to only 0.002 nm. Originally X-rays were called Roentgen rays, after Wilhelm Roentgen, who discovered them by chance in 1895. They are normally produced in an X-ray tube, which contains no air. Electrons are produced inside the tube and accelerated to extremely high speeds. When these electrons strike a target made of the metal tungsten, within the tube, X-rays are produced.

Many substances become fluorescent when struck by X-rays. If a human body is placed between an X-ray tube and a fluorescent screen, shadows of the bones appear on the screen, because they absorb X-rays more than the surrounding flesh. An object inside the body such as a swallowed safety pin, may also be found by its dark shadow. A photographic film can be used in place of the fluorescent screen. In this way, cracks and flaws may be found in metal castings.

Beyond X-rays we have the gamma rays. These emit the lowest wavelength electromagnetic radiation. Gamma rays have tremendous penetrating power. Their wavelength is so small that it is difficult to observe any wave-like properties. They appear more like particles and are often called gamma ray **photons.**

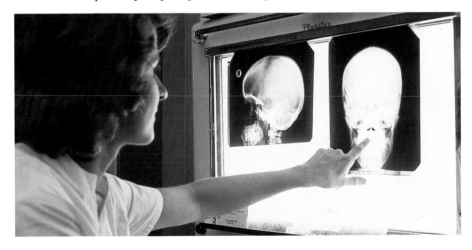

produced may be greatly increased for a short time if the substance is heated. Some types of paint are made to be phosphorescent, so that they glow for a time in the dark. Since the 1930s, fluorescent compounds have been added to some man-made fabrics used in clothing. This makes them glow slightly in sunlight, or under a UV lamp, and gives an impression of brilliant whiteness. Clean tooth enamel will also glow under UV light due to slight fluorescence.

X-ray photographs of a human skull, showing side view *(left)*, and front view *(right)*.

Type of X-ray commonly used today. A stream of electrons strikes the tungsten target and X-rays are given off. Because much heat is generated in the tube, the tungsten target rotates to prevent overheating.

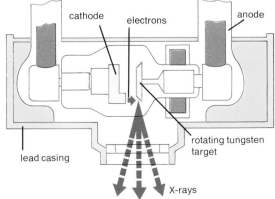

cathode   electrons   anode

lead casing

rotating tungsten target

X-rays

How a laser works

WHAT IS A LASER? Laser is one of those space-age words that people use without really understanding the meaning. You may have seen lasers used at a disco or in films.

The word laser is really a set of initials. These stand for **L**ight **A**mplification by **S**timulated **E**mission of **R**adiation. If you are still none the wiser do not worry. If you have seen a laser working you will know that it makes a very narrow, bright beam of colored light. This beam also seems to go on and on without getting dimmer. Even with a strong flashlight the beam of light spreads out and becomes dimmer in the process. A laser beam is not like this at all.

One way of describing light is to imagine it as a series of waves. Think of dropping a stone into a pool of water. Ripples are formed and the distance between two wave crests (or two troughs) is the **wavelength.** Scientists can measure the wavelength of light. Each color in the spectrum has a different wavelength, and this also can be measured.

All atoms, and the groups of atoms known as molecules, give off **radiation** when they are excited by heat, light or electricity. An example of this is seen in the sodium street lamp. In its lamp bulb are sodium atoms which are excited by an electrical discharge. When excited, the atoms give off radiation and we see this as a bright orange light.

When an atom or molecule **emits** radiation it is in a very short burst. A short burst of light like this is called a photon. In the sodium lamp millions of atoms are firing off photons without any order or timing. Thinking of water again it is like a lot of excited children in a swimming pool all splashing about. The water will be choppy but you will not see any big waves despite all their energy.

Laser light is special. The importance of a laser is that it **amplifies** light and makes it stronger. In much the same way a HiFi amplifier makes the sound louder. In a laser the atoms are all excited but fire off their photons of light in

A laser beam is a narrow, straight shaft of light – far more intense than light beams from the common spotlight. The effect, especially at night, has resulted in the use of lasers in light displays.

step with each other. A scientist calls this 'in phase'. The light produced is a very pure color because it is all of the same wavelength.

Think of the swimming pool again and imagine all the same children at one end holding the bar. If they now use just as much energy to push and pull on the bar, all together, and in time, they can make huge waves. The efforts of each of them have been **amplified** (made bigger) by acting together and keeping in time.

The famous scientist Albert Einstein worked out the theory of the laser as long ago as 1917. However, it was not until much later, in 1960, that an American scientist, Dr Theodore Maiman, working in California, was actually able to make one. His laser had a small polished ruby containing chromium atoms. It was in the shape of a rod about 5 cm long and 1 cm in diameter. It was silvered like a mirror at one end and partly silvered at the other. The ruby was surrounded by a powerful spiral flash lamp. When the flash lamp in a laser is switched on, the chromium atoms in the ruby become excited or **stimulated.** The purpose of a laser is to make as many atoms as possible give off photons to make stimulated emission.

The photons are reflected up and down the ruby by the mirrors and trigger off other excited atoms to give more photons of light. Atoms that do this emit light at the same wavelength, in the same direction, and in the same phase as the

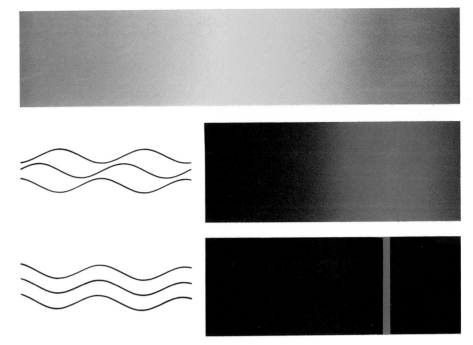

stimulating light. Because one end of the rod is only partly silvered, some of the light escapes in a narrow beam of brilliant red light. The light has been 'amplified'.

Liquids and gases are now also used in place of the ruby crystals of the first lasers. Carbon dioxide gas is used for certain high-power lasers, while others use gases such as neon and helium.

Light travels in waves. White light is made up of the colors of the spectrum, each with its own wavelength. If we look at one color, for example red, the waves it produces are similar to one another, but not 'in phase'. However, red laser light waves are in phase – following an exact and steady pattern – resulting in the sharp red beam.

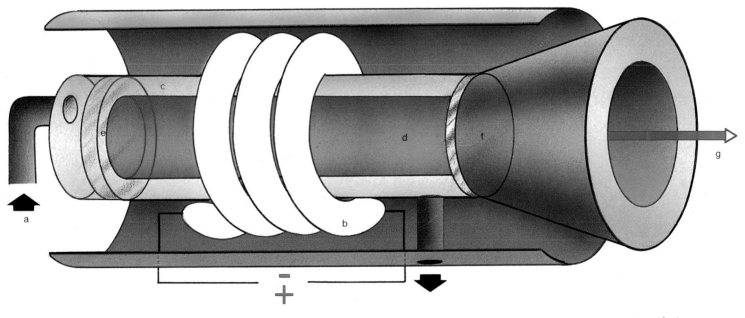

This diagram of a ruby laser shows that the theory is quite simple. Around the ruby crystal is a glass tube, containing a flow of coolant. At one end of the tube is a mirror, at the other a semi-transparent mirror. The powerful light coiled around the tube flashes and excites the atoms in the crystal, making them move around very quickly. They emit short bursts of light (photons), which reflect up and down the tube off the mirrors at each end. Eventually the activity is intense enough for a beam of laser light to escape through the semi-transparent mirror.

a   coolant
b   flash lamp
c   glass tube
d   ruby
e   mirror
f   partly silvered mirror
g   laser light

How lasers are used

THE FIRST LASER was made in 1960. Then, many people just thought of it as a new way of making a brilliant beam of colored light. But the light a laser produces is special. A laser produces a very narrow beam of light that does not seem to spread out. The light is also of a single pure color. A single color means that the light waves are all of the same wavelength. Sunlight is a mixture of wavelengths. Laser light is also **coherent.** This means it gives a very powerful beam of light.

There are now many kinds of laser. Different laser materials produce laser beams of different color and even some where the beam is invisible. The first laser used a ruby. There are now lasers which use gases and liquids to produce laser light.

The helium-neon laser is a gas laser. This type of laser can be made small enough to be carried by hand. Because a laser beam is so straight and narrow it can be used like a ruler in the sky. Construction surveyors need to mark out straight lines and make sure objects such as pylons are in line. The laser is ideal for this. When tunnelling or laying pipes underground it used to be difficult to see if the tunnel or pipes were in line. The laser beam makes this job easy. When building a skyscraper it is difficult to use a plumb line. A laser beam does not get blown about by the wind and is long enough to reach to the moon if necessary.

The laser as a cutting tool. This carbon dioxide laser is being used to cut through a steel plate. The intricate pattern calls for a tool that can cut with great accuracy – this tool does just that, and does not wear out like traditional equipment.

The true visual effect of a hologram (from the Greek 'holos' meaning whole), is impossible to see in a normal photograph. However, these two pictures show a holographic plate taken from different angles. A laser light source is needed to produce or view a hologram.

54

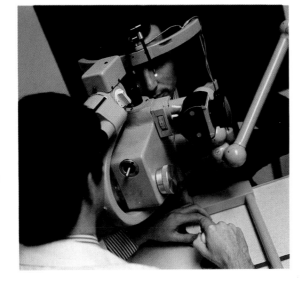

The uses of laser technology are varied and valuable. Here an argon laser is being used in eye surgery. Lasers are being used in an increasing range of surgical operations, including the treatment of tumors and brain surgery.

At discos you sometimes see a revolving ball covered with small mirrors. Hanging near the ceiling it reflects any lights shone on it. In 1976 NASA launched an earth satellite covered in mirrors. Using lasers and mathematics it has been possible to measure the shape of the earth to an accuracy of 20 mm.

There are many industrial uses for lasers. Lasers can be a source of great heat. Using a magnifying glass the sun's rays can be focused to a small spot. This spot is hot enough to set paper on fire. The beam from a laser can be focused to an even smaller and hotter spot. The high-power carbon dioxide laser is able to cut or weld sheet steel. In clothing factories cloth has to be cut according to patterns. At home you would lay the pattern on one layer of cloth and then cut it out with scissors. In a factory many layers are cut at once using a laser. The laser cuts neatly and unlike scissors never gets blunt.

In electronic circuits very thin wire is needed. This wire is made by drawing thick wire through a hole slightly smaller than itself. This is repeated with smaller holes until the right thickness is reached. The hole has to be in a very hard material so that it does not wear to a larger size. When you are making wire that is much thinner than human hair there can be problems. The wire is fed continuously through a tiny hole in a diamond. A diamond is used because it is very hard and does not wear. A laser is the best tool for drilling very tiny holes in any very hard material. Metal drills wear out and break. Lasers do not.

Perhaps the most exciting use of lasers is for **holography**, which is a new kind of photography in which the photograph is called a 'hologram', meaning a 'complete picture'. Whereas a photograph shows a two-dimensional flat picture, a hologram can do something new – it can show a 3D (three-dimensional) picture. How does it do this? An image is first recorded on to a special glass plate, a hologram plate, using laser light. To view the image, the hologram plate must be lit by means of a laser. If you look through this plate as if you were looking through a window, you will see a picture, but if you move your head a little, you will see the sides of the image as if the object were floating in space. Imagine the possibilities of holographic television where the characters are in the room with you.

There are many other uses of lasers. These range from delicate surgical work to reading the bar codes on grocery packages in the supermarket.

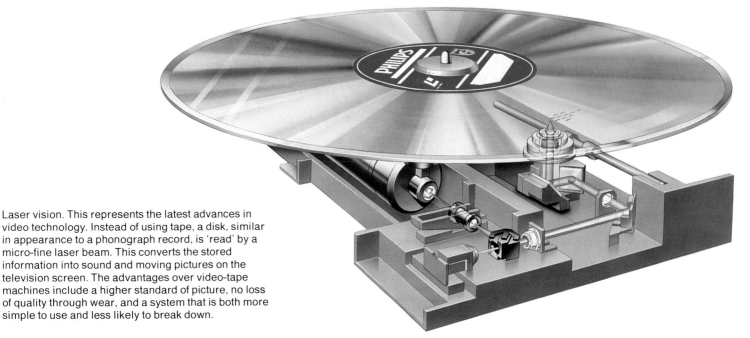

Laser vision. This represents the latest advances in video technology. Instead of using tape, a disk, similar in appearance to a phonograph record, is 'read' by a micro-fine laser beam. This converts the stored information into sound and moving pictures on the television screen. The advantages over video-tape machines include a higher standard of picture, no loss of quality through wear, and a system that is both more simple to use and less likely to break down.

Fibre optics

TELECOMMUNICATION SYSTEMS are able to carry many kinds of information throughout the world. When you use a telephone you speak into a microphone. The sound vibrations of your voice are changed into electrical signals and these signals go down a wire system to the other telephone. Here the signals are changed back into sounds by the receiver. The sound you hear in the telephone is a good copy of the voice you are listening to.

One problem in the past was the weakness of the signals because of the length of the cable. To overcome this problem, wires were made thicker. By 1900 long distance telephone wires were as much as 5 mm thick, and to make these was very costly. More recently, boosters were used to make the signals stronger.

The capacity of a channel depends upon its **band-width.** For example, a color television needs two thousand times the band-width of a telephone to transmit its signal. The medium waveband for radio broadcasting is very crowded and this is why you sometimes have difficulty in selecting the station you want. There are band-width limits for telephone cables, and only thirty telephone calls can be carried by a pair of wires made of copper.

A fibre optic telephone cable. These are now common between cities, and may soon replace the solid copper cables to the home itself. When this happens, the way is open to an almost unlimited number of communication channels into our homes.

The latest fibre optic telephone cables are a great improvement. Each cable is made up of a number of optical fibres and each fibre can carry up to 1920 telephone calls at any one time. For this reason they are rapidly replacing copper cables. A laser is used as a source of light for fibre optic telephone cable. Just as before, your voice speaking into the telephone is changed into a signal, but it is a light signal and not electrical. At the end of the cable the signal is, once again, changed back into sound. Fibre optic cables can also carry television signals and data can be passed from one computer to another.

Although these special cables are not cheap to produce, it is possible that in time every home will have its own fibre optic cable link. This will be able to carry telephone, television and radio programs. It will also be possible for the electricity and gas meters to be read without the meter reader visiting the house.

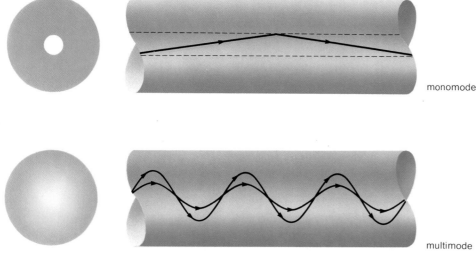

monomode

multimode

Light passing down an optical fibre can produce problems with light 'echoes' or reflections. This upsets the message being transmitted and over a long distance accuracy will be lost. A solution to the problem is the 'monomode' fibre *(top)*, which has a very thin central core preventing any internal reflection. Although monomode cable is useful, it is awkward to join two cables together because the core is so tiny.

'Multimode' fibres *(above)* have a wider core and are easier to join. Their disadvantage is that the message distorts more rapidly as it travels down the cable. This is due to internal reflection. For long distances, booster modules are required at regular intervals.

Joining optical fibres *(right)*. The glass fibre is so thin that it can be bent and rolled up. The fibre will eventually be protected by other materials to avoid risk of damage.

This experiment *(below)* clearly shows that light can be made to bend round corners. The jet of water acts in this case like the glass fibre of the optic cable. For the best effect try this in a darkened room. Fill a glass jar with water and pierce two holes in its lid (one to allow air in and the other to let water out). Place it in a hollow cardboard tube with a flashlight, making sure that the light can only escape through the hole in the jar. Then simply tip the tube so that the water starts to pour. The stream of water will light up.

How is this possible, and how does the light signal work? An optical fibre is a very long, thin glass rod. Glass is normally very brittle, but if it is melted and drawn into very thin glass fibres, like cotton candy, it becomes strong and bendable. When a light is shone in at one end of the fibre, the light stays inside and only comes out at the end. This is true even if the fibre is bent into a curve.

If you hold a stone over a pond and drop it, it will hit the water and sink. But if you throw the stone to glance off the water at a shallow angle, it will often bounce off the water into the air again. This is what happens to light in a glass fibre. The light rays strike the inside wall of the glass fibre and are reflected at a shallow angle. This is known as total internal reflection. This is how fibres can take light around corners.

In the diagram you can see how to set up a simple experiment to show how light can travel along a curved stream of water. Illuminated water fountains work in the same way by trapping light inside the jets of water.

There are a number of uses for fibre optic cable. Sometimes it is important to be able to see around corners and into dark places. An aircraft engineer may need to see inside an engine without having to take it apart. Also, a doctor may need to see inside a person's stomach without doing a surgical operation. This sort of thing can be done with a **fibroscope**. Light is passed along a fibre to where it is needed and special viewing fibres bring the image back to the viewer. The viewing fibres are arranged in a regular pattern and the picture appears like a jig-saw puzzle. For the picture to be sharp, a large number of fibres are needed. In a bundle only 3 mm square there could be as many as 100,000 fibres.

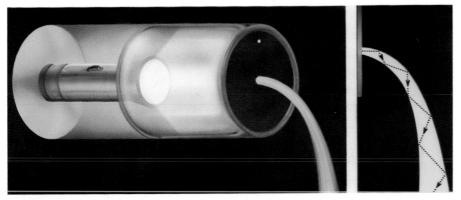

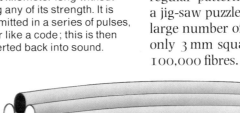

This picture *(left)* shows light at the tips of optical fibres. Light can travel along a fibre more than a kilometer long without losing any of its strength. It is transmitted in a series of pulses, rather like a code; this is then converted back into sound.

coherent bundle

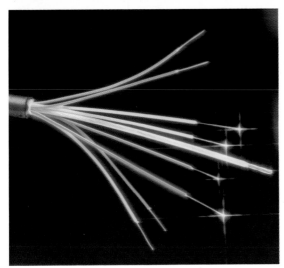

random bundle

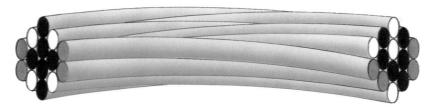

If a bundle of fibres is arranged in the same order throughout its length, a pattern or an image, can be transmitted down its length. This is known as a coherent bundle. Where the arrangement of the bundle is random, a jumbled image will result.

The miracle of sunlight

FOR CENTURIES, man has been trying to invent a machine that, once started, would continue forever without the need of fuel. This idea is called perpetual motion and is an impossible dream. A machine will only keep working if we continue to put **energy** into it. The automobile gets its energy from gasoline and your bicycle gets energy from your leg muscles.

The world is like a huge machine with plants and animals as the moving parts. The energy that drives this machine is sunlight. This light travels 150 million km across space at a speed of 300,000 km per second. Eight and a half minutes after leaving the surface of the sun, a light ray reaches a green plant on earth to start a fascinating chain of events.

Life on earth depends upon green plants. Even lions, which do not eat plants, feed upon animals that do. Plants need only water, air, **mineral salts** from the soil, and sunlight. Everything except sunlight is used over and over again, or **recycled.** In every breath you take there will be at least one **molecule** of the carbon dioxide that was breathed out by a dinosaur. Sunlight cannot be recycled, in the same way that a car cannot produce gasoline from its exhaust. The energy contained in sunlight is changed into other kinds of energy that other

Plants depend on the rays of the sun for their energy and growth. In a dense wood few plants are found at ground level, since most of the light has been absorbed by the tree cover. Where the sun reaches a clearing, many more ground plants will normally be found.

A scanning electron micrograph *(opposite)* of a barley leaf, showing stomata among epidermal cells. Magnification shown is 960 times.

A section of leaf *(opposite)* showing the various cell layers. The tough epidermis, or 'skin' of the leaf absorbs sunlight, and passes it on to the palisade cells, which contain chlorophyll. Air containing carbon dioxide is absorbed via the open stomata on the underside of the leaf.

creatures can use. Eventually the energy from the sun will pass through a whole chain of plants and animals and some of it will be returned to outer space as heat.

Plants are the basis of all life because they can trap sunlight in their leaves. They are able to do this because their leaves contain a green pigment called **chlorophyll.** This pigment is a special chemical that turns light energy into **chemical energy.** The new chemical energy can be compared to the electricity in your home which makes the electric range, the television and other things work. In the plant the chemical energy is used to make sugar molecules from water and carbon dioxide, a gas present in air. We can think of the plant needing six bottles of carbon dioxide and six of water to make one bottle of sugar and six of oxygen.

Plants are important because they lock the energy from sunlight into molecules of sugar. Animals can then use these sugar molecules as food and release the stored energy to produce movement or activity. The process by which plants use sunlight to produce sugars is called **photosynthesis.** As well as making sugar, plants also produce oxygen as part of the process. Animals need oxygen to 'burn' their food, in the same way as a fire needs oxygen to burn coal.

⇨ energy
⇦ water and minerals
⇨ carbon dioxide
⇦ oxygen

The two diagrams show a plant during daylight and in darkness. During the day sunlight acts on chlorophyll in the leaves. Carbon dioxide from the air, and water are taken in. This is converted into oxygen which is given out, and sugar (energy) which goes to feed the plant. In the dark, oxygen is taken in and carbon dioxide and water are given out.

During this 'burning' of food, or **respiration,** animals turn sugars and oxygen back into carbon dioxide and water. This completes a full circle from plant to animal and back to plant.

Photosynthesis has two reactions, one that needs light and one that does not. The **light reaction** is when the sun's energy is used to split water molecules. Water is made up of atoms of oxygen and hydrogen. In the plant, oxygen is released as a gas and the hydrogen is used with carbon dioxide to make sugar. Light is not needed to join the hydrogen and carbon dioxide and this is called the **dark reaction.**

Plant leaves are made of layers of different cells. Each layer does a certain job, like workers on the production line of a factory. The outer parts of the leaf are covered in a tough 'skin' called the **epidermis.** The top of the leaf has a clear epidermis which lets light pass through to the cells beneath. These cells are called **palisade cells** and contain chlorophyll which traps the sunlight. Below these are large, round cells with air spaces in between, rather like a piece of bath sponge. The air spaces let carbon dioxide in and oxygen out of the cells.

On the underside of the leaf are tiny holes called **stomata.** Each is surrounded by two sausage-shaped cells called **guard cells** which can open or close the hole. The stomata let carbon dioxide in and oxygen out of the leaf in daytime. When there is no light, or the ground is dry, the plant cannot make sugars. At these times the stomata close to stop water vapor being lost. If too much water escapes the plant will wilt and die.

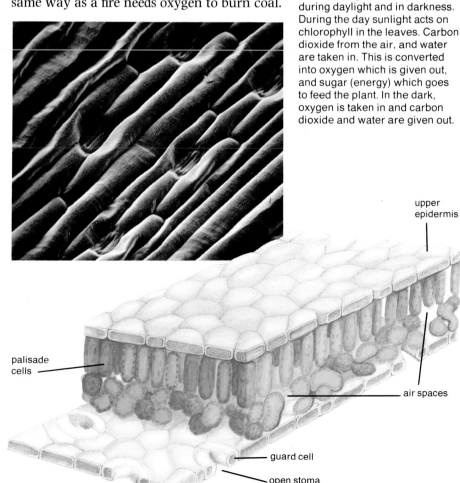

upper epidermis

palisade cells

air spaces

guard cell

open stoma

Summary

WE HAVE SEEN how Sir Isaac Newton, in 1666, passed sunlight through a glass prism and divided white light into the colors of the rainbow. This 'splitting' of light into colors is the basis of the visible light spectrum. The idea that visible light is only a very small part of a larger, continuous spectrum was first suggested by Clerk Maxwell in 1873. He called this the electromagnetic spectrum. It has been and will continue to be the adventure playground for many scientists.

Building on Maxwell's ideas, scientists could fit old and new ideas into the new spectrum. In 1800 Sir William Herschel, a British astron-omer, described the infrared part of the spectrum. This is the region we feel as heat, but cannot see. A year later, in 1801, the German scientist Johann Ritter discovered ultraviolet rays, also invisible to the human eye. Today we use infrared and ultraviolet photography in aerial survey, and in crime detection.

Towards the end of the nineteenth century scientists realized that there must be other radiations in the whole spectrum still to be discovered. In 1888 the German scientist Heinrich Hertz discovered what proved to be radio waves. We now use his name to describe all radiations with wavelengths longer than that

Scientific discovery and invention is rather like a very complicated treasure hunt. The clues are all there to be noticed and worked on; the purpose of the hunt is to unlock the secrets of nature, and use them for the benefit of mankind.

The electromagnetic spectrum is one small part of the treasure-hunt, but a very important one. The scientists who have taken part come from every nation, and the work of one scientist leads on to that of another. Even now scientists all over the world are making new discoveries.

James Clerk Maxwell
1831–1879

Wilhelm Konrad Roentgen
1845–1923

Sir Isaac Newton
1642–1727

Some explorers of the electromagnetic spectrum

1666 **Sir Isaac Newton;** showed that white light is made up of the seven colors of the spectrum. Put forward the particle theory of light.

1690 **Christiaan Huygens:** proposed the wave theory of light.

1800 **Sir William Herschel:** discovered infra-red radiation.

1801 **Johann Ritter:** discovered ultraviolet radiation, while working with silver chloride.

1820 **Hans Christian Oersted:** established the connection between electricity and magnetism.

1873 **James Clerk Maxwell:** proposed the idea of the continuous electromagnetic spectrum. He was the first scientist to realize that light is electromagnetic.

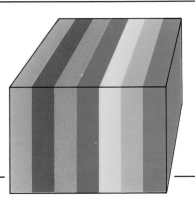

of infrared. In 1896, these radio waves were put to use in the first radio transmission by the Italian scientist Guglielmo Marconi.

By 1895, a German physicist, Wilhelm Roentgen, had extended the other end of the spectrum by the discovery of X-rays. These rays, which pass through the body, enable photographs to be taken of bone fractures or disease.

Within this framework scientists have been able to use the different wavelengths of the electromagnetic spectrum to work for them. In 1925 the first radar was tested and in 1926 the first television pictures were made. Radio, as we know it today, works within very narrow parts of the spectrum called wavebands. Each radio station has to keep to its own waveband to avoid interfering with other stations.

The radiation we call light has been put to many uses. White light is used to measure the speed of machines and 'freeze' movement in the stroboscope. The chemist and the astronomer measure the composition of a substance or of a star using a spectrometer.

One of the most exciting developments since 1960 has been the use of high energy beams of light in lasers. We use lasers to measure distances and to transmit signals to and from satellites across space. In hospitals, lasers have been used as painless scalpels in surgery of the eye and other parts of the body. An even more exciting development for the future will be the production of three-dimensional television pictures using lasers. They have already been used to make 3D pictures called holograms.

In the sphere of sight, light and color the future is full of promise. Our solar system has millions of years of sunshine left. In the future we are going to look more and more to the Sun as a source of energy. We have already come a long way towards understanding the riches in the electromagnetic spectrum. Who can tell what still remains to be discovered?

Sir William Herschel
1738–1822

Heinrich Hertz
1857–1894

Guglielmo Marconi
1874–1937

1888 **Heinrich Hertz:** discovered radio waves. He was the first to show that the frequency and wavelength of electromagnetic waves could be measured.
1895 **Wilhelm Konrad Roentgen:** discovered X-rays.
1896 **Guglielmo Marconi:** developed the first wireless telegraph. Later, in 1901 he carried out the first transatlantic wireless transmission.

1900 **Reginald Aubrey Fessenden:** transmitted human speech on radio waves for the first time.
1903 **Antoine Henri Becquerel:** confirmed the existence of gamma rays.
1908 **Hans Wilhelm Geiger:** with Ernest Rutherford, developed the Geiger counter, an instrument for measuring radioactive radiation.
1923 **Vladimir Zworykin:** invented the iconoscope, which formed the basis of the first true electronic television.

1926 **John Logie Baird:** transmitted the first television picture. Though his mechanical system was rejected, he was the first person to demonstrate that television was possible.
1931 **Karl Jansky:** developed the first true radio telescope. He founded the science of radioastronomy.
1960 **Theodore Harold Maiman:** constructed the first optical laser.

Glossary

absorb: to take in.

amplify: to increase the strength of something.

aperture: the hole in a camera, through which light passes from the *lens* to the film.

aqueous humor: clear fluid which fills the space between the *cornea* and the *lens* in the eye.

automatic: acting by itself, without the need for human control.

bandwidth: the range of *frequencies* in a channel within which a radio signal can pass.

binocular vision: seeing a single *image* with two eyes.

bipolar cell: a nerve cell from which there are two strands leading towards the brain.

blind spot: the point at the back of the eye where there are no nerve cells sensitive to light. It is where the *optic nerve* leaves the eye.

bond: the force which holds atoms together.

camouflage: protective coloring or pattern which makes animals hard to see.

celluloid: a strong plastic material that can be made into thin sheets. It is made mainly from cellulose. It burns easily.

cellulose acetate: a strong plastic, used for making photographic film.

chemical energy: the energy stored in a substance which is released during a chemical reaction.

choroid: a dark layer inside the eye which stops any light being *reflected* back.

chlorophyll: a substance found in plants which contains different *pigments*. It is used to capture the Sun's energy during *photosynthesis.*

cinematograph: the equipment used to show moving pictures.

coherent: staying together in an organized way.

color blindness: being unable to tell the difference between certain colors.

complementary color: one of a pair of colors which make white light when mixed.

compound: made up of a number of parts.

concave: with a surface curved inwards.

cone: a nerve cell in the *retina* sensitive to color. Cones are concerned with the sharpness of vision.

converge: to come close together.

convex: with a surface curved outwards.

coordination: matching movements of muscles to each other and to messages received by the senses.

cornea: the *transparent* layer that protects the front of the eye.

corpuscle: according to Newton's theory of light, a tiny *particle* moving at high speed as part of a beam of light.

countershading: coloring in animals by which their undersides, normally in shadow, are a light shade to disguise their shape.

crystalline: bright and clear, able to let light through.

curvature: the amount of curve of a surface.

cyan: a blue-green color.

dark reaction: the part of *photosynthesis* in which hydrogen and carbon dioxide are joined to make sugar.

depth: deepness down or inwards.

depth of field: the amount of the foreground or background of a photograph that is in *focus.*

develop: to treat exposed film so that the hidden picture appears as a *negative.*

developer: a mixture of chemicals in which film is soaked to change exposed silver salts into metallic silver, so that a *negative image* appears.

disk film: cassette in which single *frames* of film are arranged round a plastic wheel, instead of on a reel.

display: pattern of showy behavior in animals used to attract or warn off another animal.

electric current: the movement of free *electrons* through a conductor, such as a metal wire.

electric field: the space around an electrically charged object where it can exert a force.

electromagnetic wave: a wave combining electric and magnetic forces, spreading out through space. Electromagnetic waves include light, heat and radio waves.

electron: a *particle* in an atom, outside the nucleus, with a negative electric charge.

electronic flash: a photographic flash unit powered by electricity. The power is stored until the unit is used, when it discharges through a tube of gas to produce a bright light.

emit: to send out.

emulsion: the light-sensitive coating on photographic film and paper, made of silver salts floating in *gelatin.*

energy: the power a body has to do work.

enlarger: a special type of *projector* which makes a photographic *positive* from a *negative*, and can make the picture larger.

epidermis: the tough outer layer of a plant's leaves, stem and roots.

erect image: an image seen through a telescope the same way up as if the object were seen with the naked eye.

evolve: the process by which animals and plants gradually change over millions of years.

expose: to lay open to the effects of light.

exposure meter: an instrument that shows how the camera should be set to let in the right amount of light to take a picture.

eyepiece: the *lens* nearest to the eye in a microscope.

facet: the *cornea* covering one *ommatidium* in an insect's eye.

fibroscope: an instrument for seeing into small and awkward places, using fibre optic cable.

film speed: a measurement of how quickly a film reacts to light.

filter: a colored sheet of clear glass or plastic.

f-stop: a camera setting which shows the size of the *aperture* as it relates to the *focal length* of the *lens.*

fix: to make the picture on a photographic *negative* permanent.

fixer: a mixture of chemicals used to wash away unexposed silver salts on film, when it has been developed.

flash unit: a device which produces a very bright short flash of light. This can be timed to go off at exactly the moment when a photograph is taken.

fluorescence: the sending out of visible light from a material when a beam of light falls on it.

focal length: the distance between the center of a *convex lens* and its *focus.*

focus: the point at which light *rays* come together and an *image* appears sharp and clear.

foreshortening: drawing an object as it appears in space with lines and shapes shorter and smaller as they get further away.

fovea: the yellow spot: a small dip at the centre of the *retina* in the eye where daylight vision is sharpest. It contains only *cones.*

frame: a single picture, used in a series to make motion pictures.

frequency: the number of complete vibrations per second in a *wave.*

gelatin: a type of glue made from animal bones and skins.

greenhouse effect: heating effect when visible light passes through glass or a thick layer of atmosphere. Objects reflect it as *infrared* at a different *wavelength.* These rays cannot pass back out but heat the air inside.

guard cell: one of a pair of special cells which surround a *stoma* in a leaf and open or close it.

holography: making an *image* in three dimensions by using a split laser beam.

horizon: the part of the Earth's circumference that we can see where land and sky seem to meet.

illusion: something which is not really as it appears.

image: a picture or appearance.

impulse: a charge of *energy* which acts as a signal. The 'message' along a nerve fibre.

infrared: a ray with a *wavelength* just longer than that of red light we can see. It can be felt as heat.

instinct: a behavior pattern that does not have to be learned, but which animals are born with.

iris: the colored part of the eye, which controls the amount of light entering.

iris diaphragm: a metal shield in a camera which opens and closes to form the *aperture.* It can be adjusted to control the amount of light entering the camera.

lens: a piece of glass, or *transparent* material, with curved surfaces that bend light to bring an *image* into *focus.*

light reaction: the part of *photosynthesis* that uses sunlight to split water into hydrogen and oxygen.

luminous: radiating light.

magenta: a purplish-red color.

mammal: a fur-covered animal which is warm-blooded. It gives birth to live young and suckles them.

magnetic field: the space around a magnet where its force can work.

magnetic lines of force: lines showing the direction of a force in a *magnetic field.*

magnetism: the way in which a piece of iron can attract or repel another piece of iron or an electric conductor placed near it.

melanin: a brown or black *pigment* found in hair and skin.

mimicry: one species imitating the color, shape or sound of another.

mineral salt: a mineral needed by plants and animals to stay healthy, and in a form that can be dissolved in water.

molecule: the smallest particle of an element or *compound* that can exist by itself.

nanometer (nm): one-billionth of a meter.

negative: a reversed image produced when photographic film is developed. Light areas appear dark and dark ones light.

niche: the position of a living thing in the natural community.

nocturnal: awake and active at night, resting by day. Bats are nocturnal animals.

nucleus: the central part of an atom, containing nearly all its mass.

objective: the *lens* nearest the object being studied under a microscope.

ommatidium: one unit of the *compound* eye of an insect.

opaque: not allowing light to pass through: the opposite of transparent.

optic nerve: large nerve which carries signals from the eye to the brain.

ozone: a form of oxygen which absorbs *ultraviolet rays* from the Sun. A layer in the atmosphere prevents these rays from reaching Earth and destroying life.

palisade cell: a cell near the top of a plant leaf that contains *chlorophyll*.

parallel: always at the same distance apart. The opposite sides of a square are parallel.

particle: a very small piece of solid material.

perception: the understanding of information received through the senses.

periscope: an instrument which uses mirrors for seeing objects which are above eye-level.

perspective: the method used for drawing solid objects and scenes on paper to give an effect of distance, depth and solidity.

phosphorescence: a greenish glow of light given out by a material without heat.

photon: a small amount of light energy that can be measured.

photosynthesis: the process by which green plants capture energy from sunlight to make their food from water and carbon dioxide.

pigment: any substance that gives colour to tissues or cells in animals and plants, or can be ground to a powder to color paint and dye.

plate: a piece of glass covered with light-sensitive material, used in photography.

pole: one of the points at each end of a magnet.

pollution: the act of making the environment dirty and harmful with rubbish, fumes and waste chemicals.

positive: a picture which looks like a real view we can see: the opposite of a *negative*.

primary color: one of three colors which, when mixed, will produce any other color. For light they are red, green and blue. Primary colors of paint are red, yellow and blue.

primary rainbow: a rainbow formed when sunlight is reflected once inside raindrops.

primate: the group of *mammals* to which monkeys, apes and humans all belong.

prism: a solid shape with equal and *parallel* ends (often triangular) and sides with parallel edges.

projector: a machine which shines a bright light through *positive* film and throws the *image*, much enlarged, on to a screen.

pupil: the opening in the *iris* of the eye through which light enters. It can be made bigger or smaller.

radiate: to send out a wave of *radiation*.

radiation: a wave of energy, such as light, heat or radio energy, sent across space.

radio wave: an *electromagnetic wave* with a long *wavelength*.

ray: a narrow beam of light, and the line along which it is *radiated*.

real image: an image formed on a screen when light rays *converge* after passing through a *lens*.

receptor: part of the nervous system whose special job is to receive information from inside or outside the body.

recycle: to re-use old products to make new ones.

reflect: to send back.

reflection: light sent back to our eyes when it bounces off a surface.

refract: to bend a *ray* of light, and change its direction.

refraction: the way a *ray* of light is bent when it passes from one *transparent* material to another (eg, from air to water).

refractor: a simple telescope in which rays of light pass through a lens and the image is then magnified by a second lens.

Renaissance: a period at the end of the Middle Ages in Europe when interest in the arts was revived, and new discoveries were made.

respiration: the process by which living things use oxygen to break down their food to get *energy*.

retina: the layer at the back of the eye which is sensitive to light. It contains *rods* and *cones*.

rod: a nerve cell in the *retina* sensitive to differences between light and dark, and able to pick up small amounts of light.

satellite: a small body in orbit around another body in space. Artificial satellites circling Earth reflect radio signals to other parts of the world.

sclera: the tough, outer covering of the eye which appears as the white part.

secondary rainbow: a second rainbow formed when sunlight is reflected twice inside raindrops. It appears above the first, is fainter, and the colors are in reverse order.

shutter: the shield in a camera that opens the *aperture* for an instant to let light in.

silver bromide: a colorless silver salt used in making photographic film. It is destroyed when exposed to light, to leave metallic silver.

size constancy: the adjustment made by the brain to match what it sees with what it already knows about an object.

solar cell: a unit containing silicon which changes *radiation* from the Sun into electrical energy.

spectrum: the whole range of *electromagnetic waves*, including radio waves, heat and light, *ultraviolet* and X-rays. Also, the rainbow of colors made when white light is split by a glass *prism*.

standard lens: a lens that produces an image the same as the one we see by looking straight ahead.

stimulate: to excite, or produce action.

stoma (pl, stomata): a tiny hole in the *epidermis* of a plant leaf which lets gases in and out of the leaf. It is controlled by a pair of *guard cells*.

stroboscope: a lamp which flashes regularly at a frequency that can be adjusted. If it flashes in time with the movements of, say, a machine, the machine will appear stationary.

tear gland: an organ under the eyelid which produces tears to wash the eye.

telephoto lens: a lens that makes things seen through a camera appear nearer and larger.

thermal imaging: picking up a picture on special film of the heat given off by an object.

thermal radiation: *radiation* felt as heat.

time lapse: a type of photography in which an interval of time is allowed to pass between each *frame*. When the finshed film is viewed, movement appears to be speeded up.

transparent: able to be seen through clearly.

ultraviolet: a *ray* with a *wavelength* just shorter than that of violet light. Ultraviolet rays cannot be seen.

vacuum: an empty space with no air or any other matter in it.

vanishing point: the distant point where *parallel* lines appear to meet.

vertebrate: an animal with a backbone and skull.

viewfinder: the part of the camera you look through to see what you are taking a picture of.

virtual image: the image formed when light is *reflected* or *refracted*: it cannot be thrown on to a screen.

visible light: waves in the electromagnetic *spectrum* that humans can see.

vitreous humor: clear jelly which fills the inside of the eye between the *lens* and the *retina*.

wave: a regular up and down movement.

wavelength: in wave motion, the distance between the tops of one wave and the next.

wide-angle lens: a lens that bends more light rays into *focus* in a camera than we can see by looking straight ahead.

zoetrope: an early instrument for showing moving pictures by flashing a series of gradually changing pictures across a viewing slot.

zoom lens: a lens like a *telephoto lens*, but with which the size of the image can be changed from larger to smaller.

Index

ampere 46
aperture 38
aperture ring 38
arctic fox 33
artificial light 6
astronomical refractor 16, 17
astronomical telescope 16, 17
atoms 46, 52, 53

Baird, John Logie 61
band-width 56
barometer 8
battery 46
Becquerel, A. E. 50, 60
bee 23, 26, 27
binoculars 14
brain 7, 21, 22, 25, 28, 30, 44

camera 4, 5, 7, 20, 36, 37, 38, 39, 40, 41, 44, 45; aperture 38; aperture ring 38; depth of field 39; exposure meter 39; film 36, 38, 39, 44, 45; flash-unit 44; focus 38; f-stop 38; high-speed 44, 45; iris diaphragm 38; Kodak 37; lens 14, 15, 20, 37, 38; movie 42, 43; shutter 39; standard lens 38; telephoto lens 38; viewfinder 39; wide-angle lens 38
camouflage 32, 33; in animals 32, 33
carbon dioxide 59
cave painting 7
cell 24, 25, 59; bipolar 25; guard 59; light sensitive 24
celluloid 40
cellulose acetate 40
chameleon 33
chemical energy 59
chlorophyll 59
cine camera 42, 43
cinema 42, 43
cinematograph 42
color 4, 5, 12, 18, 19, 24, 25, 26, 27, 32, 33, 34, 35; blindness 25, 27; complementary 35; filters 35; in animals 32, 33; in light 12, 18; pigment 23, 24, 25, 34, 35; primary 25, 26, 34, 35; spectrum 18, 19, 26, 34, 35
compound eye 23
compound microscope 15, 16
concave lens 13, 14, 16
concave mirror 13, 17
cone 21, 22, 24, 25, 35
convex lens 14, 16, 17
coordination 7
cornea 21
countershading 33
Crimean observatory 17
Crivelli 29
crystalline lens 20
cyan 35

Daguerre, Louis 37
daguerreotype 37
dark reaction 59
depth 29
depth of field 39
developer 40
developing (film) 40
developing tank 40
disk-film 40
display 32, 33

Eastman, George 37, 40
Einstein, Albert 11, 53
electric current 46

electric field 46
electromagnetic radiation 46, 47
electromagnetic spectrum 47, 48, 60, 61
electromagnetic wave 46
electron 46
electronic circuit 55
electronic flash 45
emulsion 40
energy 6, 36, 58; chemical 59
enlarger 40, 41
epidermis 59
erect image 17
Euclid 10
exposure meter 39
eye 4, 5, 7, 20, 21, 30, 38; aqueous humor 21; blind spot 21; choroid 21; compound 23; cones 21, 22, 24, 25, 35; cornea 21; crystalline lens 20; farsighted 21; focus 20; fovea 25; iris 20, 21; lens 20, 21, 23; lids 21; muscle 21; nearsighted 21; omma-tidium 23; optic nerve 21; perspective 28, 29; pupil 21, 23; receptor 24; retina 21, 22, 24, 25; rods 21, 22, 23, 24; sclera 21; short sight 21; tear gland 21; vitreous humour 21
eyeglasses 15

facet 23
Faraday, Michael 46
Fessenden, Reginald Aubrey 61
fibre optics 56, 57
fibroscope 57
film 38, 39, 40, 41, 42, 43
film speed 40
filter 35
fixer 40
Fizeau 46
flash (photography) 44, 45
fluorescence 51
focal length 14
focus 14, 20, 21, 38
Foucault 11, 46
frame 42
frequency 11, 47
Frisch, Karl von 26, 27
frog 27, 32; South American tree 32
f-stop 38

Galilean telescope 16
Galileo, Galilei 16
gamma rays 51
Geiger, Hans Wilhelm 60
gelatin 40
glass 56, 57; optical fibre 56, 57
greenhouse effect 48
Gregory, James 17
guard cells 59

Hale reflector 17
Herschel, Sir William 17, 48, 60. 61
Hertz, Heinrich 46, 60, 61
high-speed photography 44, 45
holography 55, 61
horizon 28
Huygens, Christiaan 10, 11, 60

imagination 7
infrared 36, 48, 49
infrared radiation 48, 49; photography 49
insect 32, 33
iris 20, 21
iris diaphragm 38

Jansky, Karl 61
Jupiter 16

Kodak camera 37
Kohlrausch 46

laser 52, 53, 54, 55, 56, 61; carbon dioxide 53, 55; gas laser 54; helium 53, 54; helium-neon 54; holography 55, 61; neon 53, 54; ruby 53, 54; stimulated emission 52, 53; uses of 54, 55, 61
lens 14, 15, 16, 17, 20, 21, 38, 40, 43; camera 38, 39; concave 14, 16, 17; convex 14, 16, 17; crystalline lens 20; erecting lens 17; eyepiece 15; fish eye 38; objective 15, 16, 17; standard 38; telephoto 38; wide angle 38; zoom 38
Leonardo da Vinci 29
light 4, 5, 6, 7, 8, 9, 14, 15, 26, 27, 30, 34, 35, 40, 41, 52, 53, 60, 61; amplification 54; artificial 6; color in 11, 34, 35; corpuscles 11; filter 35; laser 52, 53, 54, 55, 56; ray 14, 15, 18, 58; reaction 59; reflection 8, 10, 11, 12, 13; refraction 9, 11, 14, 18, 19; scattering 50; sensitivity 36, 37; speed of 11, 58; ultraviolet 26, 36; wavelength 50, 51, 53; waves 11, 52, 53
Lippershey, Hans 16

magenta 35
magnetic field 46
magnetism 46
magnification 15
magnifying glass 15
Maiman, Theodore, Dr 53, 61
Marconi, Guglielmo 61
Maxwell, James Clerk 46, 60
medium wave 56
melanin 36
microphone 56
microscope 15
microwave 49
Milky Way Galaxy 6
mimicry 32
mineral salts 58
mirror 8, 12, 13, 16, 17; concave 13; convex 13; in telescope 16, 17
molecule 36, 58
monkey 22
moth, peppered 33
motion pictures 42, 43
movie camera 42, 43
movies 43

nanometer 48
negative 40
Newtonian reflector 17
Newton, Isaac 11, 17, 18, 60
nucleus 46

objective lens 16, 17
Oersted, Hans Christian 46
ommatidium 23
optic nerve 21
optical illusion 20, 30
optical fibre 56, 57
ozone 51

palisade cells 59
peacock 32
peppered moth 33
perception 30
periscope 12
perpetual motion 58
perspective 28, 29; fore-shortening 29; illusion 29; Renaissance 29; size constancy 28; vanishing point 28
phosphorescence 51
photography 36, 37, 38, 39, 40, 41, 42, 43, 44, 45, 49; daguerreotype 37; developing 36, 37 40, 41; electronic flash 45; high-speed 44, 45;

infrared 49; photographic emulsion 40, 41; photographic film 40, 41, 44; photographic plate 37; pin-hole camera 37; silver bromide 36; time lapse 45
photon 11, 52, 53
photosynthesis 59
pigment 23, 24, 25, 34, 36, 59
pin-hole camera 37
pipe-vine swallowtail 32
plants 58, 59
pollen 32
pollution 33
positive (film) 40
primary colors 34, 35
primate 7
prism 26, 48
projector 43, 44
Ptolemy 10
pupil 21, 23

Ra 6
radar 61
radiation 52, 61
radio 56, 60, 61; broadcasting 56
radio waves 46, 60, 61
rainbow 19
real image 14
reflecting telescope 16, 17
reflection 8, 10, 11, 12, 13
refraction 9, 11, 14, 18, 19
refracting telescope 16, 17
respiration 59
retina 21, 22, 28
Ritter, Johann 50, 60
rod 21, 22, 23, 24
Roentgen, Wilhelm 51, 61

satellite 5, 49
Saturn's rings 16
Scheele, Carl 50
sense 4, 30
shutter 39, 43, 44
sight 4, 5, 6, 7, 8, 30
signals 56
silver bromide 36
silver salts 40
snakes 32
South American tree frog 32
space telescope 17
spectrum 18, 19, 26, 34, 35, 48, 50, 51, 53, 60, 61; colors of 18, 19; electromagnetic 47, 48, 60, 61; infrared 27, 48, 49, 60; ultraviolet 26, 50, 51, 60; violet 50; visible 18, 19, 26, 34, 35, 48
speed of light 46, 58
spice-bush swallowtail butterfly 32
standard lens 38
stomata 59
stroboscope 44
sugar 59
sun 4, 6, 8, 9, 36; burn 36, 51; Ra 6
sunlight 4, 6, 8, 18, 19, 36, 50, 58, 59
sun-worship 6, 8
sunspots 16

Talbot, William Fox 37
telecommunication 56
telephone 56; cable 56; microphone 56; signals 56; wire 56
telephoto lens 38
telescope 16, 17; astronomical 16, 17; Crimean observatory 17; eyepiece 16; Galilean 16; Hale reflector 17; lens 16, 17; reflecting 16, 17; refracting 16, 17; space telescope 17; Yerkes telescope 17

television 4, 5, 56
thermal imaging 48, 49
thermal radiation 48
time lapse photography 45
Torricelli 8

ultraviolet 26, 36, 60

vacuum 8
vanishing point 28
viewfinder 39
virtual image 14, 17
vision 22, 23; animal 22, 23, 26, 27; binocular 22; birds' 22, 23; color 26, 27; field of 22; nocturnal 23

Wollaston, William 50
wasp 32
waveband 56; medium wave 56
wavelength 11, 19, 26, 47, 48, 49, 50, 51, 52, 53, 60, 61
Weber 46
wide-angle lens 38

X-rays 51, 61

Yerkes telescope 17

zoetrope 42
zoom lens 38
Zworykin, Vladimir 61